Students and External

DATE DUE

TWAYNE'S WORLD AUTHORS SERIES
A Survey of the World's Literature

SPAIN

Janet W. Díaz, Texas Tech University

EDITOR

Ignacio Aldecoa

TWAS 529

Ignacio Aldecoa

IGNACIO ALDECOA

By ROBIN FIDDIAN
University College, Galway

TWAYNE PUBLISHERS
A DIVISION OF G. K. HALL & CO., BOSTON

Published in 1979 by Twayne Publishers,
A Division of G. K. Hall & Co.
All Rights Reserved

Printed on permanent/durable acid-free paper and bound
in the United States of America

First Printing

Frontispiece photograph of Ignacio Aldecoa by Müller

Uo

Library of Congress Cataloging in Publication Data

Fiddian, Robin.
Ignacio Aldecoa.

(Twayne's world authors series ; TWAS 529 : Spain)
Bibliography: p. 168–75
Includes index.
1.   Aldecoa, Ignacio—Criticism and interpretation.
PQ6601.L253Z66   863'.6'4   78–23220
ISBN 0-8057-6370-8

Contents

About the Author

Robin Fiddian holds the degrees of M.A. and Ph.D. from the University of Edinburgh. He has taught at the University of Strathclyde and at University College, Galway, where he is Statutory Lecturer in the Department of Spanish. He has a special interest in Spanish literature of the nineteenth and twentieth centuries, and has published a number of articles concerning the Generation of 1898 and the contemporary novel of peninsular Spain. These have appeared in *Modern Language Review, Forum for Modern Language Studies, Romance Notes, Iberoromania,* and *Revista de estudios hispánicos.* Dr. Fiddian has also contributed to the volume entitled *Ignacio Aldecoa — A Collection of Critical Essays.* As the recipient of various awards, he has visited Spain frequently for the purpose of research.

Preface

The death of Ignacio Aldecoa in November 1969 meant the loss of a major talent in Spanish literature of the post–Civil War period. Aldecoa belonged to a generation of writers who gave a new direction to Spanish prose fiction in the 1950s and 1960s. The aim of the present study is to determine the specific nature of his contribution to that collective endeavor, through an examination of the qualities inherent in his personality and writings. Our task has been facilitated by the recent wave of academic publications concerning Aldecoa. A volume of essays published in the summer of 1977 by the University of Wyoming bears witness to the complexity and diversity of his writings as well as to the gathering momentum of critical interest displayed in them throughout Europe and America.

We begin by projecting Aldecoa's life and work against a backdrop of historical and literary trends, as many of his literary creations cannot properly be understood without reference to their historical context, and are, in fact, striking examples of the shaping of literature by history. This is not to say that they can be dismissed as period pieces since, as will be seen, the best of them possess qualities which transcend both temporal and geographical limits.

While a general outline of Aldecoa's life is easily given, many intimate details still await discovery and documentation. The absence of a coherent body of autobiographical reminiscences about his childhood and adolescence is a particular obstacle to the complete understanding of his personal and professional development; the acquisition of such information is an enterprise for future students of Aldecoa. As far as the author's adult years are concerned, valuable information has been provided by his widow and close friends. His own compositions also reflect his personality with varying degrees of immediacy, and we have turned particularly to his journalistic essays in search of authentic insights into his attitude to social and human issues.

The monumental changes which have overtaken Spanish society in the years since Aldecoa's death have to some extent simplified the task of establishing an adequate literary perspective. However, certain dogmatic and conflicting views have still not been satisfactorily reconciled, with the result that only an eclectic attitude to stated critical standpoints may provide an accurate picture of Aldecoa's position as regards movements and trends such as tremendism, costumbrism, social realism, and existentialism.

The bulk of our study is taken up with an analysis of Aldecoa's fiction. The four novels are accounted for in chapters 3–6. The next four chapters center on Aldecoa's short stories which many critics feel represent his major claim to celebrity. In individual analyses of over fifty items we attempt to discover the peculiarities and foundation of his craft. Since Aldecoa's work in poetry and the travel genre has suffered from widespread neglect, we consider it at some length, along with a miscellaneous volume entitled *Neutral Corner* (chapters 11–12).

In an interview with Luis Sastre, Aldecoa once voiced a firm, if partial, opinion about the function of literary criticism. He advised that "The first thing to do is to find out what the author has set out to achieve; then, see if he succeeds. Without these two premises, there can never be true criticism." Fidelity to a purpose is certainly one important criterion for judging an author's work. In our attempt to gauge Aldecoa's success, we have drawn widely on his declarations to the press in which he defined his general principles and stated what he intended in specific instances.

For the purpose of establishing an all-round critical perspective, it has frequently been necessary to review certain *idées reçues* in circulation since Aldecoa emerged as a figure of note. These accepted notions refer to his position vis-à-vis other writers of his generation, the dominant values in his work, and the nature of his craft. While seriously attempting to evaluate Aldecoa's work in relation to a Spanish tradition of realism and in relation to the achievements of other writers who were his contemporaries, we have been guided above all by the desire to assess what is unique in his literary make-up. We have inquired into the quality of his thought and feeling, the verisimilitude of his representation of human and social reality, and the artistic effectiveness of his choice of technical means. An appreciation of aspects of technique and style, both in poetry and prose, helps to illuminate Aldecoa's development to a state of maturity which was interrupted only by death.

Preface

It has proven expedient to translate original source material in prose into English, except when illustrating stylistic and rhetorical features. In such cases and when analyzing poetry, the original Spanish version is also quoted.

ROBIN W. FIDDIAN

University College, Galway, Ireland

Acknowledgments

I am indebted to Domingo Pérez Minik and José Arocena of Tenerife in the Canary Islands who, from personal acquaintance with Ignacio Aldecoa, were able to give me valuable biographical information and advice about the interpretation of his work. I am grateful to Doña María Teresa de Aldecoa for providing details about her brother's childhood. I owe a particular debt of gratitude to Doña Josefina Rodríguez de Aldecoa who granted me access to her late husband's private library and files, allowed me to reproduce three of his poems here, and gave generously of her time and attention. Finally, I wish to thank the Royal Irish Academy and University College Galway for financial support, and to acknowledge bibliographical assistance from Hipólito Esteban Soler of the University of Santiago de Compostela in Spain.

Chronology

1925   José Ignacio de Aldecoa born 24 July in Vitoria in the province of Alava.

1936   Writes first accomplished story and publishes first newspaper article. Remains in Vitoria during Spanish Civil War.

1942   Proceeds to the University of Salamanca. Contributes to student publications.

1945   Moves to Madrid as a student of history. Involved in the *postista* movement.

1947   Publishes first volume of poetry, *Todavía la vida.*

1948   Publishes first short stories in student journals.

1949   *Libro de las algas,* his last venture in poetry.

1951   Takes part in *misiones pedagógicas* with his fiancée, Josefina Rodríguez.

1952   March, marries Josefina Rodríguez. Begins to write commercially for journals including *Guía, Indice, Clavileño,* and *Cuadernos hispanoamericanos.* Finalist for Gijón Prize with "Ciudad de tarde."

1953   Involved in foundation and management of *Revista española.* December, wins Youth Prize with "Seguir de pobres."

1954   Takes part in *jornadas literarias* around La Mancha. October, a daughter, Susana, is born. Runner-up in the Saturday Novel competition with "El mercado" and for the Planeta Prize with his first recognized novel *El fulgor y la sangre,* the initial volume of a projected trilogy entitled "La España inmóvil."

1955   May, takes part in the *jornadas literarias* to Alta Extremadura and writes a poetic account of the journey. July–August, sails the Great Sole fishing area. Publishes *Espera de tercera clase* and *Vísperas del silencio,* incorporating material old and new.

1956   February, *Con el viento solano,* the second volume in the "La España inmóvil" trilogy.

1957   January–February, visits Canary Islands as reporter for *Arriba.* Wins Virgen del Carmen Prize with his third novel, *Gran Sol.*

1958 July, visits Ibiza with wife and child. October, family leaves to spend seven months in United States.

1959 *El corazón y otros frutos amargos,* a volume of stories.

1960 Aldecoa's mother, Carmen Isasi, dies. First adaptation of one of his stories to film.

1961 February–March, visits Canary Islands. Publishes *Cuaderno de godo, Un mar de historias, Caballo de pica*, and *Arqueología.*

1962 June, travels to Paris and Munich with a group of socialists. Visits Poland with his wife. Publishes *El país vasco* and *Neutral Corner.*

1963 Among signatories to a letter of protest submitted to Minister of Tourism and Information. Publishes *Pájaros y espantapájaros.*

1964 Visits United States a second time.

1965 *Los pájaros de Baden Baden. With the East Wind* successfully adapted as a film.

1967 *Parte de una historia.*

1968 *Santa Olaja de acero y otras historias,* an anthology.

1969 Involved in various projects in literature, television, and cinema. Ignacio Aldecoa dies, 15 November.

CHAPTER 1

Aldecoa's Life and Times

I *The Early Years*

JOSÉ Ignacio de Aldecoa was born in Vitoria, the capital of the northern province of Alava, on the evening of 24 July 1925. He was the first child of Simón de Aldecoa and Carmen Isasi; a second child, a girl named María Teresa, was born two years later. Simón de Aldecoa was an artisan of the middle class who ran a family business in industrial decoration and restauration inherited from his father, Laureano de Aldecoa. According to the limited information available, the young José Ignacio — affectionately called Iñaki in the home — enjoyed a happy and lively childhood marred only by his experience of school.

In interviews with the press in the 1950s, Aldecoa contrasted his relaxed family upbringing in the early thirties with the formal restrictions on education in the period after the Civil War. He documented his love of nature and in particular his passion for the sea. Throughout his childhood he would be taken for holidays to the coast of Vizcaya (Biscay) and Santander, where he was able to indulge his love of fishing and swimming. A fascination for railway engines and steam trains was another sign of his childhood romanticism. Indoor pursuits included the usual games with toy soldiers, a perverse interest in dissecting animals with his sister and, more relevant to this study, a formidable devotion to collecting and reading books and listening to stories. José Ignacio could read by the age of four. By the mid-1930s his library included a wide range of classics, many published in the Espasa Calpe series of that period, and stories of travel and adventure by authors such as Jules Verne and Salgari.

A major formative influence was his maternal grandmother, María Pedruzo, with her tales of the Carlist War of the 1870s and the Cuban disaster of 1895–1898. These historic events are recalled

13

in Aldecoa's first novel and in his story "La humilde vida de Sebastián Zafra" ("The Humble Life of Sebastián Zafra"). The impact of other stories about smuggling and banditry is echoed in Aldecoa's boast that some of his forefathers had been "shepherds and smugglers."[1] He was never to lose interest or respect for cowboy tales, cheap thrillers, detective stories, and other subgenres of popular literature. His first attempts at writing imitated tales of the sea: "I started with Robinsons and Salgaris," he declared.[2] At eleven years of age he wrote his first story of the sea, and published his first article, about bullfighting, in a local newspaper.

The young José Ignacio was further influenced by contact with a group of artists who gathered at his parents' house in number 42 Calle Postas. Manuel García Viñó has remarked on the artistic achievements of José Ignacio's uncle, Adrian Aldecoa, who won local and national awards for his paintings.[3] Aldecoa maintained and developed an interest in the pictorial arts until the end of his life. He was later to associate with painters such as Manuel Mampaso in Madrid, and devoted some essays to the subject. His familiarity with painting also had a determining effect on his descriptive style.

José Ignacio received his primary and secondary education between the ages of five and seventeen from the Hermanos Marianistas in Vitoria. Though a Catholic institution, the school was less strict in religious orientation than those run by other orders. The loss of his faith at the age of twelve nevertheless caused complications in Aldecoa's education, to the extent that his widow has described his experience at school as "disastrous" and "precarious."[4] Aldecoa was a poor student who rebelled against authority. His insolent, rebellious spirit is portrayed in the autobiographical tale "Aldecoa se burla" ("Aldecoa Has a Laugh"). The text of an interview with a journalist of *La Hora* further illustrates his mischievous adolescence; it recounts his first illicit drink, in a tavern called "The Anarchist," and playful insults directed at the other sex.[5]

On the same occasion, Aldecoa recalled an incident involving some children fighting in the school playground in 1936. This event would later inspire the story "Patio de armas" ("Courtyard of Arms") which provides valuable information about the historical background to this period of Aldecoa's life. Set in a provincial school in the Basque provinces during wintertime, the story documents the occupation of Vitoria by troops of the German Condor

Legion who came to Spain to support the Nationalists at the end of October 1936. Infamous for its role in bombing the Republican towns of Durango and Guernica, the Condor Legion was for some time in the spring of 1937 based at Vitoria and other northern Nationalist airfields (German presence in the grounds of the school which Aldecoa attended is attested in a letter to this author from his sister, María Teresa de Aldecoa).

The Spanish Civil War had broken out in July 1936. The rising began at Melilla, in Spanish Morocco, on the evening of Friday, 17 July and quickly affected other colonial centres there. It spread to the mainland in two waves throughout the eighteenth and nineteenth, until by 21 July over half of Spanish territory was under rebel control. In the north, from the Atlantic coast of Galicia to the western Pyrenees, only Asturias, Santander, and the two Basque provinces of Biscay and Guipuzcoa remained loyal to the Republican government, of which Azaña was president and José Giral prime minister, having succeeded Casares Quiroga and Martínez Barrio.

The city of Vitoria, in the Basque province of Avila, fell to the Nationalists without difficulty but the Republican front lay no more than fifteen kilometers away to the north at Villarreal. It was not until April 1937 that Nationalist forces pushed the Republican lines back toward Bilbao, finally capturing the city in June of that year. The Aldecoa family, in Vitoria when the rebellion began, was obliged to postpone their summer holiday in Santander. Simón de Aldecoa was a member of a small local nationalist group, Basque Action, which aligned with the forces loyal to the Republic. Caught in a Nationalist zone, he and one of his brothers escaped detention on two occasions during the early days of the war. With the enforcement of order, the children's education was administered almost as normal in Vitoria, though not without interruptions for the burial of relatives killed at the front, as depicted in "Courtyard of Arms."

Other works by Aldecoa besides "Courtyard of Arms" document the social and political unrest in Spain during the 1930s and the wartime period. Examples include "Las piedras del páramo" ("Stones of the Wilderness"), "Young Sánchez," in which a fleeting reference is made to the battle for Madrid in the university city, "Fuera de juego" ("Offside"), where a character enumerates the battles in which he fought, and others. But the most notable is Aldecoa's first novel, *El fulgor y la sangre* (*Blood and Lightning*), which evokes the spirit of proletarian dissent during the *bienio negro* of November 1933 to February 1936, including the revolt of the Asturian miners in October 1934, the frequent strikes and electoral upheavals leading up to the rebellion, the outbreak itself as experienced in both rural and urban areas, the ubiquitous cycles of atrocities and reprisals, popular dissatisfaction with Azaña, and the siege of Madrid.

The effect of the war on the young Aldecoa, eleven at the time of the outbreak and almost fourteen when fighting ended in April 1939, is difficult to assess, as there is no reference to the subject in any of his personal or autobiographical declarations. His statement of 1950 that he had no memories concerning politics,[6] is a consequence of the fact that writers were obliged to practice "self-censorship" ("autocensura"). Since neither Aldecoa nor his family suffered directly as a result of the war, it is probably correct to assume that the historical circumstances of his early youth served as a source of artistic inspiration, without giving rise to emotional trauma or personal resentment. However, one cannot underestimate the devastating spiritual effect of living in what Aldecoa's close friend, Ana María Matute, termed "an atmosphere of a world in crisis."[7]

II   *Student Years and Adulthood*

As little is known about Aldecoa's life in the three or four years immediately after the Civil War as in the period between 1936 and 1939. He continued to read prolifically and widely — French poetry caught his interest at this time — but enjoyed only those subjects at school which catered to his adventurous, imaginative spirit. He now found the cultural atmosphere in the city of Vitoria oppressive in its provinciality and, upon completion of his secondary studies, left for the University of Salamanca where he spent two years studying *comunes,* the general subjects which in Spanish third level education serve as a basis for subsequent specialization.

Education in Spain at this time was completely determined by the politics and economics of the Franco regime. As Chief of the Armed Forces, Head of State, and head of all successive governments, General Francisco Franco was able to shape a totalitarian political structure incorporating Catholics, Falangists, Monarchists, and the Military who had supported the Nationalist cause. The Falangists enjoyed considerable temporary influence between 1939 and 1945, but then suffered a diminution of power in the formation of a new cabinet which was to remain in office until 1951. Throughout the 1940s, Spain was isolated from the rest of Europe, first while World War II was fought, and then as a result of ostracism by the victorious democratic Western powers. In this decade there began the dour task of reconstructing a country drained of manpower and resources, bereft of an adequate system of transport and energy, and weakened by low levels of agricultural and industrial production. The Spanish government's economic policy was designed to achieve self-sufficiency through state intervention and protection, with acquiescence of the work force guaranteed by the national syndicalist program of the Falange. Stagnation, inflation, rationing, and a flourishing black market were the consequences of this policy until the turn of the decade.

Life in Spanish universities and other cultural establishments took place against this background. One commentator describes the first stage of postwar education, between 1939 and 1951, as "a long stationary phase" marked by dogmatism and interference;[8] another prefers to characterize it as "a very grave regression (rather than mere stagnation) in the cultural life of the country."[9] Falangist principles were influential in the propagation of the new regime's ideology and values. Young Falangists were in charge of the only permitted student organization, the Sindicato Español Universitario (Spanish University Syndicate). Each university rector was required to be a member of the Falange and every teacher to swear allegiance to the regime. The majority of the staff, according to Salvador Giner, were "Catholics of extreme traditionalist orientation."[10] Dogmatism and censorship created a climate of intellectual repression.

While privileged to figure among the 0.145 percent of the population then registered at a Spanish university, Aldecoa was not impressed by the formalities of university life at Salamanca. Carmen Martín Gaite, one of his fifteen classmates and herself a future novelist, has indicated that while other students attended lectures with reverence and assiduity, Aldecoa freely went his own way, associating with a broad range of people outside the university and indulging his interest in popular culture. The same writer has recorded Aldecoa's enthusiastic response to the popular artist, Rambal, who played at the Liceo in Salamanca during his presence there as a student.[11]

Aldecoa's preference for popular, as opposed to academic, culture is reflected in his writings of that period. In poetry and prose he drew on the conventions of epic narrative and balladry, favoring themes of danger and adventure which he treated in a lively and ironic way. These themes were destined to exercise a permanent appeal on him. A critical article on elements of fantasy and mystery in the work of E. T. A. Hoffman, Edgar Allan Poe, and the nineteenth-century Spanish poet, Gaspar Núñez de Arce, demonstrated a similar bias against erudition. The range of Aldecoa's interests is shown by a second article contributed to *Cátedra,* a monthly magazine published by the Students' Union in Salamanca, treating activities of the university theater group there.

Involvement in extracurricular affairs did not prevent José Ignacio from achieving success in his examinations, and in 1945 he proceeded to Madrid to specialize in American history. While he was never to complete his studies, the years spent as a student in Madrid favored the further development of his personality and literary ambitions. At the university he came into contact with a group of aspiring writers and artists including the prose writers Jesús Fernández Santos, Rafael Sánchez Ferlosio, Fernando Guillermo de Castro, and Carmen Martín Gaite, the dramatists Medardo Fraile, Alfonso Paso, and Alfonso Sastre, and the painter Manuel Mampaso. Fernández Santos has given a revealing account of his generation's experience: "For many of us [namely, Fernández Santos, Sánchez Ferlosio and Aldecoa] life at university consisted of attending a few classes, passing two or three exams, holding long conversations in the bar, and making a number of friends. There was little talk of politics, and although there was some activity it was not all that noticeable; as I say, times were hard." In such an environment Aldecoa and his companions found opportunities to discuss issues of life and literature. Fernández Santos continues: "We began to influence one another. . . . We read some worthwhile books which (at least in my case) echoed our ideas and aspirations in a vague sort of way."[12] Such gatherings, or *tertulias,* also centered around the Pensión Garde, in the Pasaje de la Alhambra, where Aldecoa shared accommodation with the painter Pedro Bueno and the poet Carlos Edmundo de Ory; the Nicaraguan poet Carlos Martínez Rivas was another member of this circle.

In his first year in Madrid Aldecoa was involved in the controversy surrounding the *postista* movement. This was founded in January 1945 by Carlos Edmundo de Ory, Eduardo Chicharro, and

Silvano Sernesi, as an irreverent challenge to existing conceptions of literature and the plastic arts. It was meant to be a revival and extension of the avant-garde as embodied previously in futurism, cubism, surrealism, and ultraism. Carlos Edmundo de Ory's definition of *postismo* as "invented madness"[13] conveys both the exultation of imagination and feeling, and the preeminence of technical experimentation which are its principal characteristics. There was much naivety and affectation in this short-lived movement, but in the context of Spanish culture in the mid-1940s *postismo* represented an understandable impatience with conformity and an attempt at Europeanization. In a stern refutation of criticism leveled against the *postistas* by a student, Jesús López Medel, Aldecoa identified himself with them: "We *postistas* (simple and good-hearted folk, honorable and pleasant to deal with)...," and defended *postismo* as being open-minded and "Europeanizing."[14] The priority of European over national concerns is reaffirmed in another, otherwise unexceptional, article of his which appeared in a university journal, *Trabajos y días,* in 1949.

It is ironic that Aldecoa's enthusiasm for the *postista* cause should scarcely be corroborated in his creative writings of the time. In December 1947 he published a volume of poetry entitled *Todavía la vida* (*Life Still Goes on*). Although one poem is dedicated to Carlos Edmundo de Ory and written in the *postista* manner, the remaining eighteen betray the influence of *garcilasismo,* a poetic movement and style which flourished between 1943 and 1946 and against which *postista* criticism was in the main directed. Aldecoa's preference for a traditional mode of lyric poetry is reemphasized in a second volume, *Libro de las algas* (*Book of the Algae*), which he financed himself and saw published in 1949. Although he continued to write poetry in the following years, this was his last publication in the genre. From the end of 1948 onward he cultivated stories and short novels.

The years 1949 to 1959 were to be the most productive in Aldecoa's career as a writer of prose fiction. By the end of the 1950s, with some sixty stories and three novels to his name, he had established himself as a writer of note inside Spain and had begun to attract critical attention abroad. His first stories appeared in Madrid periodicals including *La Hora* and *Guía,* of the Spanish University Syndicate, *Juventud,* "The Weekly Magazine of Spanish Youth," and literary publications such as *Correo Literario* and *Clavileño.* Also associated with *La Hora* were Jesús Fernández

Santos, Fernando Guillermo de Castro, Medardo Fraile, and
Alfonso Sastre; José María de Quinto was literary critic for the
paper, and Manuel Mampaso provided illustrations for stories by
the various authors in both *La Hora* and *Correo Literario*. Aldecoa
was shortly able to form anthologies of his narratives: *Espera de
tercera clase* (*Waiting Room, Third Class,* 1955) comprised five
items, *Vísperas del silencio* (*The Eve of Silence*) of the same year,
ten, and *El corazón y otros frutos amargos* (*The Heart and Other
Bitter Fruits,* 1959), eleven.

The stories ranged from fantasy and fable, through burlesque,
parody, and satire, to reflections on the state of society and sensitive studies of the human condition. Those of social intent ranked
high in the critics' estimation, as can be seen by their placing in
competition for literary prizes. Aldecoa was a finalist for the Gijón
Prize in 1952 with "Ciudad de tarde" ("Evening City"), and
runner-up in The Saturday Novel competition of 1954 with "El
mercado" ("The Market"), an abridged version of a short novel.
In December 1953 he won the Premio Juventud (Youth Prize) with
"Seguir de pobres" ("Continuing Poverty"), an indictment of
conditions in rural Spain. This prize was awarded by a panel
reported to have consisted of Pedro de Lorenzo, Gabriel Elor-
riaga, Jesús Fragoso del Toro, and José Antonio Elola.[15] Gaspar
Gómez de la Serna, who has testified to a slightly different composition of the board, described "Continuing Poverty" as "completely representative of that mood of critical appraisal and disconformity with the structures of Spanish society" which characterized
an emerging generation of writers, known collectively as social realists, whose chief aim was to denounce the social and economic
conditions prevalent in Spain throughout the 1940s and 1950s.[16]
These were times when the working and lower middle classes suffered badly. Although from the beginning of the fifties American
military aid gave a boost to the economy, providing conditions for
industrial expansion, and although the renewal of diplomatic relations with most Western powers paved the way for increased foreign trade, there was no effective economic planning in Spain until
1959. The neglect of agriculture had especially harmful consequences. The living standards of the rural proletariat were
depressed, and many families abandoned the land. Internal migration to the cities created a crisis in urban population and housing.
"Continuing Poverty" is a particularly eloquent treatment, in
artistic terms, of this social and economic hardship. Other stories

which point up Aldecoa's attention to social problems are "Solar del Paraíso" ("Paradise Lot"), "El mercado" ("The Market"), "La urraca cruza la carretera" ("The Magpie Flies over the Road"), and "Vísperas del silencio" ("Eve of Silence"), where the themes expressed are, respectively, the exploitation and vulnerability of the proletariat, the unequal distribution of wealth and welfare, migration, and urban poverty including the inadequacy of housing.

Aldecoa's first novel appeared in 1954 and made a considerable critical impression in that *annus mirabilis* of Spanish fiction. *Blood and Lightning* has consistently been regarded, along with three other works by members of the second generation of post–Civil War novelists, as a major contribution to the revival of the genre in Spain at that time. The other novels were *Los bravos* (*The Wild Ones*) by Jesús Fernández Santos, *Juegos de manos* (*Sleight of Hand*) by Juan Goytisolo, and *Pequeño teatro* (*Little Theatre*) by Ana María Matute. Aldecoa contested the prestigious Planeta Prize in October 1954 with *Blood and Lightning* and was judged runner-up to his close friend Matute. He wrote a sequel entitled *Con el viento solano* (*With the East Wind*) in less than twelve months, publication taking place in February 1956. The significance of the two novels, parts of a projected but unfinished trilogy called "La España inmóvil" ("Motionless Spain"), was seen to lie in the author's transcendence of topical subject matter and in the quality of his observation and artistic transformation of Spanish reality. *Blood and Lightning* was a fictional study of the Civil Guard, Spain's rural paramilitary police force; *With the East Wind* was broadly concerned with the position of the Gypsy community in Spanish society. Both books represented technical and stylistic achievements which earned them the description "classical." A third novel, *Gran Sol* (*Great Sole*), which appeared in 1957, won two major literary prizes, the Virgen del Carmen of that year and the significant Premio de la Crítica (Critic's Prize) of 1958. Many commentators misread *Great Sole,* underestimating the extent of Aldecoa's art. In Spain only Lorenzo Gomis, writing in *El Ciervo,* and Baltasar Porcel Pujol, in *Papeles de Son Armadans,* demonstrated any intuitive appreciation of the novel's symbolism and other poetic qualities.[17] Otherwise, realism and technical expertise were the criteria used for assessing the book's worth.

At the end of the 1950s Aldecoa was accorded feature interviews in literary journals such as *La Estafeta Literaria, Crítica,* and

Indice. On one such occasion, in May 1959, he intimated that he
had already started work on a second novel of the sea as a follow--
up to *Great Sole* and that he was planning another, "the novel of
my intermediate generation."[18] The first work eventually material-
ized some eight years later as *Parte de una historia* (*Part of a
Story*); the second never developed beyond the stage of a project,
although Aldecoa decided that its title would be "Años de crisálida" ("Chrysalis Years"). In the same interview he claimed to
have ready for publication the final volume of his "Motionless
Spain" trilogy. At that time it was called "Los pozos" ("The
Wells") and was supposed to feature an aspiring bullfighter,
Antonio Jiménez, who had played a minor role in the first chapter
of *With the East Wind.* A short story of the same title about bullfighting was later included in the volume *Pájaros y espantapájaros*
(*Birds and Scarecrows*). William J. Grupp claims that the appearance of a novel by Angel María de Lera on the same topic prevented Aldecoa from publishing "Los pozos" in full.[19] Though
apparently frustrated in his immediate desire to treat the theme of
tauromachy in the extended form of the novel, he preserved the
long-term ambition to do so until his death.

   Aldecoa's emergence as a literary figure did not bring immediate
economic benefit. As he was to state in 1965, "It is very difficult
for a writer to survive in Spain when, as a rule, taking a year to produce a novel, you receive only thirty-five to fifty thousand pesetas
[between five and seven hundred dollars at the rate of exchange in
1965]. That is not enough to live on."[20] The market and rewards
for short stories were even less secure. At the time of publication of
his first novel, Aldecoa had a wife and child to support. He had
met Josefina Rodríguez, a research student in education at the
Consejo Superior de Investigaciones Científicas (Higher Council of
Scientific Research) at the end of 1950, and the couple married in
March 1952. A daughter, Susana, was born in October 1954. Aldecoa turned to commercial journalism for a vital source of income in
the early and mid-fifties. He wrote regularly for student publications, daily newspapers, and popular magazines, contributed
reviews and essays to serious literary periodicals, and did occasional work for the radio station, Voz de la Falange (Voice of the
Falange).

   For one year, starting in June 1952, he wrote a monthly column for
Guía. According to an editorial announcement in the June issue, he
would "comment on the most unusual and entertaining news about stu-

dents and graduates all over the world." Most of the pieces were, indeed, entertaining but ephemeral. One article critical of methods for teaching school children bore the authentic mark of remembered personal experience. Another took the form of an educated appreciation of Manuel Mampaso's paintings of the sea; it is also of interest for confirming Aldecoa's firsthand experience as a sailor.

Throughout 1955 he consigned articles to a press agency for distribution to provincial newspapers such as *El Adelanto* of Salamanca, *Diario de Burgos, El Diario Palentino* of Palencia, and *Las Provincias* of Valencia. These articles represent his personality and interests more authentically than the glosses in *Guía*. His admiration for heroic and dangerous living comes out in a report on the real exploits of a Texas firefighter. Two articles display his sensitivity to social issues. One is a lament on the destruction of Castilian folklore brought about by ever-increasing rural emigration, while the other discusses the changing rhythm of life in urban society and recalls Charlie Chaplin's film *Modern Times*. Aldecoa addressed himself to the topic of popular literature in two other pieces. He reminisced about stories of piracy and adventure on the high seas which satisfied a human need for vicarious excitement, and he identified with Walter Mitty, the James Thurber creation, whose imaginative and dignified challenge to institutional monotony makes him a universal symbol of individualism. The question of man's propensity to imitate the experience of literary characters is also raised; Aldecoa treated this theme, which has been universally appropriated by writers of fiction since Cervantes, in all of his novels and in stories including "Los vecinos del callejón de Andín" ("The Folk from Andín Lane") and "Un buitre ha hecho su nido en el café" ("A Buzzard Has Made its Nest in the Café"). Lastly, from 23 January to 22 February 1957, Aldecoa was special correspondent for the Madrid daily, *Arriba*, in the Canaries, visiting all seven major islands with the photographer Pastor and, in the number for 1 February, he reported on catastrophic flooding in La Palma. The descriptive pieces produced during this assignment were later refashioned into a booklet, *Cuaderno de godo* (*A Goth's Notebook*).

During the years 1952–1954 Aldecoa wrote commercially as well as creatively for the literary journals, *Clavileño, Cuadernos Hispanoamericanos,* and *Indice.* He contributed two compositions in the travel genre to the "Paisajes y costumbres" ("Landscape and Customs") section of *Clavileño.* He reviewed a number of books, including one volume of poetry, *El hombre es triste* (*Man is Sad*) by Marcelo Arroita Jáuregui, two novels translated from the American, *Requiem para una monja* (*Requiem for a Nun*) by William Faulkner and *El arpa de hierba* (*The Grass Harp*) by Truman Capote, an essay by the Nicaraguan, José Coronel Urtecho, and two studies of Pío Baroja and Dostoevsky by the respective authors, José Luis Castillo Puche and Luis de Castresana. The review of *Man is Sad* reveals Aldecoa's enthusiasm for the rehumanized poetry of the time; those of *Requiem for a Nun* and *The Grass Harp* display his precise and up-to-date acquaintance with literary currents outside Spain; and his remarks concerning Dostoevski and Faulkner exemplify the intuitive basis of his response to literature. In the way of essays, he published "Los novelistas jóvenes americanos" ("Young American Novelists"), an informed survey of current trends in that field. An item in homage to Baroja provides further evidence of his romantic attitude toward the sea dn indicates his sense of identity as a Basque whose spiritual affinity was with the Cantabrian and Atlantic Ocean rather than the Mediterranean. Two articles signed "I. A." and attributable to Aldecoa, pass stern judgment on Spanish cultural attitudes and complain of poverty and provincialism in Spanish fiction of the time.

A further critical and semicommercial venture in which Aldecoa was involved in the early fifties was the launching of *Revista Española*. Rafael Sánchez Ferlosio, Alfonso Sastre, and Aldecoa were entrusted with the task of administering this periodical by Antonio Rodríguez Moñino, editor of the Castalia publishing house and later member of the Royal Academy of the Spanish Language. The first number of *Revista Española* came out in May 1953 with two thousand copies in print; circulation dropped to five hundred copies by the end of the year, and the sixth and final number appeared in April 1954. It was primarily a journal for the publication of short stories and literary and art criticism by writers of Aldecoa's generation. Juan Benet, Luis de Castresana, Carlos Edmundo de Ory, Jesús, Fernández Santos, Medardo Fraile, Carmen Martín Gaite, José María de Quinto, and Rafael Sánchez Ferlosio all contributed. Besides acting as one of the editors, Aldecoa published two of his own stories and a review of Sastre's play, *Escuadra hacia la muerte* (*A Squad Heading for Death*), which he commended for expressing "the uncertainty and despair of man today."[21] This comment is a telling indication of his conception of the artist as one who articulates an imaginative response to the sensibility of his age.

Literary *tertulias* and travel were two important spheres of activity for Aldecoa at this time. He and his wife met with other writers in Madrid cafés including the Abra, Capitol, Castilla, Comercial, Gijón, and Lyons. Fernández Santos recalls meeting Aldecoa in the Gijón during the days of *Revista Española,* and visiting his house in El Paseo de la Florida near the Manzanares River; the Aldecoas moved to Blasco de Garay in 1956, to a flat occupied to this day by Josefina Rodríguez. The couple also met with Gaspar Gómez de la Serna at the Capitol, and with a group consisting of Manolo Diez Crespo, Eusebio García Luengo, Francisco García Pavón, and Fernando Guillermo de Castro at the Comercial in La Glorieta de Bilbao. García Pavón has attested to Aldecoa's skill in mimicking those who accompanied him in these *tertulias.* He also mentions the latter's habit of taking bicarbonate of soda as treatment for a stomach ulcer which caused him great discomfort from 1956 onward.[22] A less frequent literary associate of the time was the Catalan critic José María Castellet, who presented Ignacio with a copy of his study *Notas sobre literatura española contemporánea* in June 1955.

Aldecoa traveled widely in the 1950s. He accompanied Josefina Rodríguez on over a hundred *misiones pedagógicas* between 1951 and 1953. These missions had begun under the Second Republic in 1933 as a means of facilitating education and promoting cultural life in deprived and backward areas of Spain. The second wave was intended as a continuation of those enlightened principles. Aldecoa also took part in the *jornadas literarias* of 1954 and 1955, organized by the Departamento de Cultura de la Delegación Nacional de Educación (Cultural Department of the National Delegation for Education). Writers and artists joined in the *jornadas* to discover the natural and historical grandeur of the Spanish regions and to report on their travels. Aldecoa went around La Mancha in 1954 with a group including Miguel Delibes, Jesús Fernández Santos, Eusebio García Luengo, and Rafael Sánchez Ferlosio, but did not contribute to the collection of articles resulting from that journey. He accompanied some sixty other writers on the trip to Alta Extremadura between 18 and 22 May, 1955, following the route Madrid-Plasencia-Coria-Cáceres-Trujillo-Oropesa-Madrid, and wrote a short, impressionistic piece, "Urgente viaje de retorno" ("An Urgent Return Journey"), for the volume *Alta Extremadura   Libro de Viaje (Alta Extremadura   A Travelog).* Francisco García Pavón, Gaspar Gómez de la Serna, and Alejandro Núñez Alonso figured among the other eighteen contributors.

Two journeys which Aldecoa made independently provided him with background material for his novels. He visited the area around Talavera and Maqueda which is the setting for most of the action of *Blood and Lightning* and *With the East Wind,* and in the summer of 1955 he sailed the Great Sole fishing area. Having registered with the maritime authorities in Santander, he boarded the *Puente Viesgo* at Gijón on 25 July. The round trip, including a visit to Bantry Bay on the southwest coast of Ireland, lasted until 18 August. Aldecoa started writing *Great Sole* immediately upon his return. His next major trip was to the Canaries at the beginning of 1957. In July 1958 he took his family to the Mediterranean island of Ibiza, to which they would return on holiday in subsequent years. The award of a grant to Josefina Rodríguez for her research in education enabled the Aldecoas to spend the winter of 1958 and the following spring in the United States. During this seven-month period, Aldecoa traveled around the East Coast states, lecturing on his work and contemporary Spanish literature to university audiences at Yale, Columbia, and Brynn Mawr. Living in New York was an exhilarating experience for both Ignacio and Josefina Aldecoa, who responded enthusiastically to the immense range of cultural activities and human experience which that city had to offer.

III   *The Last Decade*

Shortly after the family returned from the United States, Josefina Rodríguez founded Estilo, a private school for children between the ages of two and seventeen. This enterprise had a decisive influence on Aldecoa's position as a writer, removing financial pressures and guaranteeing the conditions in which to pursue his literary career without unwelcome distractions or obligations. Until his death in 1969 he was able to write, lecture, and travel with relative freedom.

His creative writing in the 1960s was confined mainly to stories and short novels. *Caballo de pica (The Picador's Mount),* which came out in 1961, contained nine new compositions along with four previously published items. *Arqueología (Archaeology,* 1961) and *Pájaros y espantapájaros (Birds and Scarecrows,* 1963) were by and large mediocre collections of extant material, but *Los pájaros de Baden Baden (The Birds of Baden Baden,* 1965) was an impressive book. It contained four narratives of intermediate length and was

the last complete volume of mature and original stories which Aldecoa published before he died. In *Santa Olaja de acero y otras historias* (*Saint Eulalia of Steel and Other Stories*, 1968) he did no
more than collect fifteen popular items from existing editions in a
new anthology. One individual story, "La noche de los grandes
peces" ("The Night of the Big Fishes"), appeared in *La Nación*, a
Buenos Aires newspaper, in 1969. *Tierra de nadie* (*No Man's
Land*), a posthumous volume of 1970, contained only one piece not
published before. Finally, two original, unpublished compositions
from 1965 and 1968 were included in a complete edition of Aldecoa's stories which Alicia Bleiberg prepared in 1973.

Social reality was still the basis of Aldecoa's narratives in the
1960s. As far as class issues are concerned, he now tended to
satirize the bourgeoisie instead of denouncing the industrial
exploitation and social deprivation of the lower classes as in compositions of the previous decade. Alicia Bleiberg has related this
shift of emphasis to the changing situation in Spanish society at
that time.[23] The sixties were a time of rapid social and economic
change in which Spain became industrialized and urbanized by
modern standards. The population of Madrid rose from two and a
quarter million in 1960 to over three million in 1970; there occurred
a general improvement in living standards, accompanied by a consumer revolution. The move in Aldecoa's stories away from indict-
ments of poverty and inequality to descriptions of bourgeois and
tourist high life in, for example, "Ave del paraíso" ("Bird of Paradise") and "Al margen" ("On the Sideline"), is symptomatic of
that overall transformation. While social themes were a constant
inspiration, Aldecoa also took as subjects for his stories universal
aspects of human experience such as loneliness, frustration, illusion, apathy, and despair.

His activity in other genres was less conclusive. The only novel he
produced in the sixties was *Part of a Story* (1967), the second volume in his projected trilogy of the sea. Set on an island in the
Atlantic ocean, it was inspired by his visit to the Canaries in 1961.
The amount of time required to complete the work — six years — is
an indication of the increasing difficulty Aldecoa experienced in
preparing and executing a full-length novel. At the time of his
death he was engaged in two fictional projects: he persevered with
Chrysalis Years and, according to a statement made in April 1969,
was planning a novel entitled *Naufragios y comentarios* (*Shipwrecks and Commentaries*) after two historical documentaries by a

sixteenth-century Castilian explorer, Alvar Núñez Cabeza de Vaca.[24] He continued writing travelogues as an expression of his interest in the regions and countryside of Spain. *Cuaderno de godo* (*A Goth's Notebook,* 1961) documented his earlier visit to the Canary Islands as a newspaper correspondent. In *El país vasco* (*The Basque Country,* 1962) he reported on his native region, and during his last months he became involved as a script writer for a projected series of television programs on Spanish rivers. His enthusiasm for the world of boxing took literary form in a unique book, *Neutral Corner* (1962). Based on firsthand acquaintance with the gymnasia and rings of Madrid, it was both documentary and epic. Lastly, during this period he wrote a small number of essays and papers on literary subjects of which the only one published was *Un mar de historias* (*A Sea of Tales,* 1961). Here Aldecoa collated all the references and conclusions he had drawn from his readings of stories about the sea. *A Sea of Tales* is at the same time illustrative of influences on his work. An identical inventory of titles and characteristics appeared in a brief prologue to a volume of stories by Jules Verne translated and published in 1969.

Literature of the sea was one of Aldecoa's favorite themes. He lectured to audiences in Spain and abroad on it and other subjects such as contemporary Spanish fiction, "The Short Story in the U.S.A.," and "The Beat Generation." He was invited to address cultural circles, for example, at Seville in November 1960, Santa Cruz de Tenerife in March 1961, when returning from the nearby island of La Graciosa, and Ibiza in the summer of 1963. He gave lectures in the American Universities of Indiana, Purdue, Illinois, and Pittsburgh in 1964, and at Aix-en-Provence in southeast France on a number of occasions during the 1960s.

There were other motives for travel. In the summer of 1962 Aldecoa and his wife went to Poland to receive the royalties on a translation of *With the East Wind;* they first had to collect visas in Paris, as diplomatic relations between Spain and Poland did not exist at the time. Just prior to this, Aldecoa had accompanied Dionisio Ridruejo, Fernando Baeza, and other socialist figures of moderate stature to Munich, where a congress of democrats opposed to the Franco regime met on 7 and 8 June. There is no great significance in Aldecoa's attendance at the assembly of the European Movement. He went along with Ridruejo's group out of friendship and an adventurous spirit of inquiry, not because he subscribed to any specific political doctrine. As Ridruejo commented some years later, "Ignacio was, without a doubt, the least political of all of us, but the little adventure provided him with some excitement and he was in good humor throughout."[25] This is a fair assessment of Aldecoa's political stance. Gaspar Gómez de la Serna's inference that, as a young man, he was a dissident Falangist like Ridruejo and Antonio Tovar, is disputed by Josefina Rodríguez and remains unproved. The fact that, in the late forties and fifties, he wrote for organs of the Spanish University Syndicate and the Falangist newspaper, *Arriba,* and that he worked on the radio station, Voice of the Falange, is not remarkable in view of the political constraints on professional journalists and writers at that time. Alfonso Sastre has argued that only people holding "anachronistic," "dogmatic," or "sectarian" opinions would have construed his own activity, and that of writers like Aldecoa, as "politically ambiguous" or as "collaboration with the régime." Sastre objects, with cutting irony, that "It was our good fortune to be caught up in the theoretical legacy of the Civil War, with all its implications for strategy and tactics."[26] Any alleged "collaboration" was the result of pragmatism.

A further assertion by Ridruejo that he and Aldecoa "shared a common viewpoint on social and political problems,"[27] may be taken as an indication that Aldecoa's stance was, if anything, that of a socialist and upholder of democratic values. He was never affiliated with any political party or organization, but remained a man of personal convictions who responded to human considerations more than to political issues. However, he would sign collective letters and petitions in defense of fundamental liberties. A document sent to the Minister of Information and Tourism, Manuel Fraga Iribarne, on 30 September 1963, expressing concern about reports of torture in Spanish prisons, bore his signature along with those of many intellectuals, including Ana María Matute, Alfonso Sastre, and Antonio Buero Vallejo, and the film directors Juan Antonio Bardem and Victor Erice. He also signed a petition to the same minister in Marsh 1965 requesting recognition of the democratic rights of students and staff at Madrid University, after some disturbances there.

A field with which Aldecoa developed close connections in the sixties was the cinema. In 1954 he and Josefina Rodríguez had written an amateur film script entitled *Cuatro esquinas (Four Corners).* In the following decade Spanish cinema became an area of expansion. One of Aldecoa's closest friends was Rafael Azcona, who

composed the scripts for two films directed by the Italian, Marco
Ferreri, *El pisito* (*The Little Flat,* 1959), and *El cochecito* (*The
Little Car,* 1960). Jesús Fernández Santos worked at the Instituto
de Investigaciones y Experiencias Cinematográficas (Institute of
Film Research and Practice), in collaboration with Jaime Camino
and Mario Camús. Camús took one of Aldecoa's stories, "Young
Sánchez," and his novel, *With the East Wind,* adapting them to the
screen in 1960 and 1965 respectively; he won the Griffith Prize in
Spain for the second venture. Two other stories, "El silbo de la
lechuza" ("The Owl's Hoot") and "Fuera de juego" ("Offside"),
were adapted by Pedro Gil Paradela for television and shown in
February 1968 and November 1969. Aldecoa showed his understanding of the film medium and his satisfaction with Camús's
interpretation and adaptation of his work, in an interview the text
of which appeared in *Griffith* at the end of 1965.[28] He also
acknowledged the influence of the cinema on his writing.

Jesús Fernández Santos and Eusebio García Luengo have both
recorded their impressions of Aldecoa in the last weeks of his life.[29]
His personality seemed to combine vitality with fatalism. On the
one hand, he preserved all the vigor, independence, and thirst for
experience which had been his most essential qualities. He returned
to the world of bullfighting, attracted as ever by the prospect of
risk, adventure, and heroism; Domingo González, known in bullfighting circles on Domingo Dominguín, was his host and companion on many visits to ranches and rings. On the other hand,
Aldecoa was prone to bouts of melancholy and presentiments of
death. His health was not good. A penchant for whiskey and cigarettes only aggravated his stomach ulcer. The late story "Un corazón humilde y fatigado" ("A Heart that is Humble and Tired")
reflects his morbid obsessions and carries disturbing autobiographical undertones. In the story, a child called Toni is con-
valescing after a heart attack, ominously aware that his mother had
died of the same condition. Like his own mother nine years earlier,
Ignacio Aldecoa died of a heart attack on the afternoon of Saturday, 15 November 1969, at the age of forty-four. Although this was
one year short of the age which he had once arbitrarily specified as
the point at which a writer· attains literary maturity,[30] his own
achievements in the short story and novel had already secured him
lasting recognition.

CHAPTER 2

The Literary Context

I General Trends in Contemporary Spanish Fiction

COMMENTATORS of Spanish literature of the post–Civil War period generally accept that major developments took place in the field of prose fiction at the beginning of the 1950s, due to the emergence of a new generation of writers known as the "mid-century generation" or the "new wave." The members of this generation shared a common birth date which critics have set arbitrarily between the two extremes of 1922 and 1936, and consequently experienced the Civil War as children or adolescents. All were conditioned by the autarkic environment of the 1940s and attendant constraints on social, political, educational, and literary activity. They were conscious of forming a "lost generation" divorced from a cultural tradition and heritage. Italian neo-realist literature and cinema, and translations of works by such figures as William Faulkner, Ernest Hemingway, and Jean-Paul Sartre influenced them in the early fifties. Inspired to write primarily by a sense of moral duty, many conceived of their role in terms of a historical mission. They drew their themes from contemporary social reality and consistently treated them in a spirit of disconformity and protest. Choosing realism as the dominant mode, they created fictional worlds whose structures and features were modeled recognizably on the reality of contemporary Spain. At the same time, many writers of the mid-century generation experimented with narrative and structural techniques of fiction, in such a way that their work represented a departure from established practice. For Gonzalo Sobejano the novelty of this realist aesthetic resides in the fact that "It goes beyond costumbrist observation and nineteenth-century descriptive analysis by purporting to give an objective representation, in a concentrated artistic form and centered on social and historical reality."[1] Rodrigo Rubio confirms that the

31

"realistic content" of the new novel was expressed in "innovatory forms."[2]

Ignacio Aldecoa shares many fundamental characteristics with the writers of his generation. Some are of a circumstantial nature, namely, his date of birth, experience of the Civil War, education in an era of autarchy, and receptivity to external literary and cinematic influences. Others have to do with his general principles as a writer. Writing was naturally a vocation for him and an enterprise involving conscientious planning: "We are here to create literature in response to our deepest convictions and experiences," he said, adding that "The fact that we may not succeed in bringing it to fruition need not prevent us from 'viewing' it from afar. So, planning my career as a novelist is a question of professional ethics, or rather a vocation, for me."[3] He was committed to truth as a moral imperative, not an epistemological category. He postulated a goal, the education and salvation of the helpless and ignorant: "People have a very hard time in this world, and not only in Spain. Some entertain hopes and wait consciously for some improvement. Others, the majority, wait in a state of unconsciousness. A long process of education is required to save these people."[4] He held that an author has many potential missions "ranging from documenting reality to protesting about it," and believed that "a novelist can assume a historical mission through the medium of literature, by fulfilling his aesthetic ideal insofar as he is able."[5]

Aldecoa's novels and stories were inspired by his direct experience and contemplation of social reality. He was intimately familiar with the geographical, professional, and social spectrum of Spain, and set out to give literary recognition to those sectors which he believed other artists traditionally neglected. It was concern for this "almost unpublished reality," as he called it,[6] which prompted him to plan a number of trilogies. The first, "Motionless Spain," was to deal with the experience of civil guards, Gypsies, and bullfighters in rural Spain, the second was to be concerned with the lives of fishermen and sailors, and the third would focus on miners and steelworkers. In fact, he managed to write only four of the projected nine volumes.

Aldecoa's work is simultaneously realistic and social. He claimed that "I am a writer who can be included unequivocally in the category of realism, or in what we generally understand by that term. I suppose I am a social writer because my concerns are basically social, and even if they were not, I should still be so, because all literature is social."[7] To adopt a more precise criterion, his books meet the basic requirements set out by Pablo Gil Casado and Gonzalo Sobejano for classification as "social literature." Gil Casado contends that "We shall call a novel 'social' only when it purports to expose the stagnation in society, or the injustice and inequality reigning there, and when it does so with the purpose of criticizing those conditions."[8] For Sobejano, a literary work may be designated as "social" only "if its central aim, as felt and expressed at the core, is collective justice."[9] When asked what he wrote against, Aldecoa answered "Against injustice."[10] A reading of "The Crow Flies Across the Highway" or "Continuing Poverty" shows his intentions in this regard. José Corrales Egea's statement that "Aldecoa is not completely insensitive to the historical and social environment"[11] is a gross underestimation of his social conscience and commitment.

The author's experimentation with new techniques and his revision of stylistic norms make him typical of his generation which transformed the inherited aesthetic. Ronald Schwartz concurs with Juan Ignacio Ferreras' assessment and classification of a representative range of writers including Ana María Matute, Elena Quiroga, José Luis Castillo Puche, Rafael Sánchez Ferlosio, Juan Goytisolo, Jesús Fernández Santos, Juan García Hortelano, and Aldecoa, as the principal practitioners of "transformed realism." Schwartz writes: "The novelists who use this style employ 'traditional' realism as their inspiration, however through greater narrative skill and new experimental writing techniques, they explore the problems of modern Spain, bringing their readers up to the absolute present moment...."[12] Aldecoa sympathized with those critics who lamented the persistence of outmoded conventions in the Spanish novel of the early 1950s. One such person wrote despairingly in 1953: "The Spanish novel is anachronistic.... In a few days' time someone among us will discover realism of the type Juan Valera used [in the 1880s]."[13] In the same year Aldecoa lamented "the narrowness of vision which is the result of our isolation from [recent] trends in fiction."[14] Insisting on the importance of "rhetoric" and the need for adequate technique, he contributed to the revitalizing of the Spanish novel by introducing new modes of structure and narrative presentation and by transcending the methods of costumbrism and tremendism.

Costumbrism was a Spanish literary movement with a long history which took definitive shape in the first half of the nineteenth

century. In the words of one of its commentators, "The characteristic of *costumbrismo* was its interest, not in observed reality as a
whole, but in those aspects of reality which were both typical of a
given region or area in Spain and at the same time pleasingly picturesque and amusing."[15] There was in Spanish prose of the
post–Civil War period a revival of costumbrism with which Aldecoa has often been identified. He indeed chose many topical themes
for his novels and stories, but did not merely copy the conventional
or exalt the picturesque. As his widow explains, "He wanted to
adopt a human perspective of topical subjects, to see the other side
of things."[16] In 1955 Aldecoa outlined his intentions: "The bad
thing about topics in our literature is that they have always been
treated in isolation. My aim is to group them together and give
them the greatest possible significance. I believe I am on solid
ground here because I am talking about people and places of which
I have firsthand experience."[17] Critics have acknowledged his success in excluding the folkloric and picturesque from, for example,
the two volumes of his trilogy "Motionless Spain." He received
similar recognition for overcoming the limitations of tremendism, a
manner of writing which enjoyed diffusion and notoriety in Spain
in the 1940s and early 1950s. Tremendism portrayed brutal, vulgar,
and grotesque aspects of reality, implied a pessimistic view of man,
and relied on caricature and deformation in style and technique.
There has been a tendency to associate it with the European movement of existentialism. Drawing on this view, Pablo Borau has
related Aldecoa to "Spanish existentialism, otherwise called
tremendism."[18] William Grupp and Gaspar Gómez de la Serna
have disputed the assertion, however.[19] Aldecoa inherited some
stylistic norms of tremendism, but he rejected it outright as a moral
and aesthetic system. Ana María Navales reports that, when asked
his opinion of tremendism, Aldecoa dismissed it as "a series of
extreme situations which cannot be justified."[20]

II   *Aldecoa and the Neo-realists*

Notwithstanding these substantial points of coincidence between
Aldecoa and other prominent members of his generation, several
commentators have accorded him a marginal position in an over-
view of the contemporary Spanish novel. Recognizing the need for
discrimination, Hipólito Esteban Soler, in a comprehensive analysis of Spanish fiction in the fifties and sixties, has distinguished

four groups within the mid-century generation: neo-realists, social realists, metaphysical realists, and critical realists.[21] Esteban Soler's distinctions are deliberately schematic and pretend only to provide a working model of analysis. According to him, the neo-realists include Jesús Fernández Santos, Ana María Matute, Rafael Sánchez Ferlosio, and Aldecoa; they started publishing between 1948 and 1954. Their work is characterized by a dual concern for social and personal aspects of human experience, a predilection for intimate themes, particularly that of childhood, and innovation in artistic treatment. The social realists include Juan Goytisolo, Antonio Ferres, Armando López Salinas, Alfonso Grosso, Jesús López Pacheco, and Juan García Hortelano; with the exception of Goytisolo, who may be considered to span the two groups of neo-realists and social realists in chronology and style, these writers first published between 1958 and 1961. They were highly politicized and vocal dissidents who subordinated literary to social values, eschewing the technical and stylistic refinement of the neo-realists. The metaphysical realists include Antonio Prieto, Carlos Rojas, Andrés Bosch, and Manuel García Viñó; although Prieto published his first novel in 1955, it is in 1958 and 1959 that representative works of this group appeared. The metaphysical realists rejected what they saw as a superficial and sterile conception of concrete reality, and chose instead to cultivate an intellectual type of fiction concerned with abstract, transcendental issues. Lastly, the critical realists include Luis Martín Santos, Juan Benet, and "evolved" writers like Juan Goytisolo and Alfonso Grosso whose work developed apace with innovatory trends in Spanish fiction from the mid-1960s on. The aim of the critical or dialectical realists has been to break down fundamental myths of Spanish culture and lay bare the contradictions inherent in Spanish society. Forsaking the mimetic and objective techniques of the social realists, they have produced works as subversive in form and style as they are in content.

Esteban Soler's classification of Aldecoa as a neo-realist alongside Ana María Matute, Jesús Fernández Santos, and Rafael Sánchez Ferlosio is a reassertion of the view which Eugenio de Nora and Julio Martínez de la Rosa originally proposed and to which Darío Villanueva and Manuel García Viñó have given further support and currency.[22] Aldecoa himself made some relevant declarations. In his essay "A Personal View of Spanish Fiction Today" he identified himself with what he called "the intermediate generation,"[23] a group consisting of Jesús Fernández Santos, Juan Goytisolo, Rafael Sánchez Ferlosio, Alfonso Paso, and Alfonso Sastre. A slight anomaly in Aldecoa's scheme was the decision to class Ana María Matute with Miguel Delibes, Juan Gironella, Carmen Laforet, Ignacio Agustí, and Sebastián Juan Arbó, in a preceding generation of older novelists who came to the public's attention between 1945 and 1950. A second document indicates his acceptances of the rubric "1954 promotion" for himself and his companions: "We are a promotion set apart and without antecedents, but very Spanish." He added that the group was united in its search for "a novel of realistic and lyrical qualities in present-day Spain."[24]

What primarily distinguishes Aldecoa's work and that of the other members of this "promotion" from the overall trends in the novel of the fifties and sixties is precisely a quality of *intimismo* on which many critics have remarked. In 1952 José María de Quinto had articulated the wishes of many young writers when he called for "an art of human values with a foundation in social reality."[25] In 1961 Francisco García Pavón praised the fusion of social content and emotion in Aldecoa's work and argued that he diverged from the social realists by virtue of sensibility.[26] Gaspar Gómez de la Serna took up this thesis and proclaimed Aldecoa a writer "with the fine sensibility of a humanist,"[27] whose aim was to capture the essence of human intimacy.

Aldecoa himself defined "reality in literature" as "the tempering of fact with the author's sensibility."[28] The preeminence of sensibility meant that Aldecoa's perspective of reality was at variance with that of the social realists. While sympathizing with their mood of criticism and protest, he did not subordinate art to political doctrine, nor did his depiction of society conform to a one-dimensional scheme dictated by ideology. In terms of technical and stylistic treatment he also differed. Concerning objectivism, the preferred mode of the social realists, he confided to Miguel Fernández Braso: "It interests me, certainly, but it is nothing I am very enthusiastic about."[29] And his prose was more ambitious, more refined, and richer in poetic devices than that of the generality. Stories like "The Heart and Other Bitter Fruits" and "On the Other Side" illustrate Aldecoa's practice of treating social themes provocatively while at the same time evoking human intimacy. This dual quality, along with his subtle, allusive technique and precise, lyrical prose, aligns him with the neo-realists of his "promotion."

Another defining characteristic of his work, shared to a large extent by the neo-realists, is recourse to archetypal symbolism. Recent studies have acknowledged this aspect of Rafael Sánchez Ferlosio's work;[30] it has been established that Ana María Matute has drawn consistently on biblical sources in her conception of character, situation, and plot;[31] Juan Goytisolo's first two novels, *Sleight of Hand* and *Duelo en el paraíso (Sorrow at Paradise House)*, also exemplify a figurative procedure. Aldecoa openly deploys this typological symbolism, which never degenerates into allegory, in all but the first of his novels, through *Neutral Corner,* and in many stories and poems. Resonances from epic literature, the Bible, classical mythology, and folklore extend the imaginative scope of his work, and raise his themes to the level of universality. He also exploits archetypal symbolism to express his personal world view.

III *Distinctive Characteristics*

A classification of Aldecoa with other authors of the time in which he lived must not impair the reader's appreciation of his distinctive characteristics. Aldecoa's own references to "my intermediate generation" and "our promotion" are balanced by firm denials of affiliation to any group. His assertion that "The truly creative writer is on his own, completely and unquestionably on his own"[32] is borne out by the distinctiveness of his world view and by his own particular conception and execution of his works.

For Aldecoa possessed a personal world view which was an extension of his temperament and sensibility. In May 1959 he told an interviewer: "At present I am not an optimist. I hope to reach a state of serenity, but doubt whether I shall ever be optimistic. I shall reach a state of serenity, which is different from the resigned acceptance of oneself and one's surroundings."[33] And in 1968 he remarked with similar ambiguity: "I am a nihilist by nature, but believe in the future, even though no positive solutions can be guaranteed."[34] He conceived of the novel, and fiction in general, as "a vehicle for searching for one's self, and an attitude to the world about us,"[35] and saw his own work as "responding clearly to my conception of life and death."[36] His novels and stories from *Blood and Lightning* to *Part of a Story* and "A Humble and Tired Heart" bear witness to an abiding pessimism. Implicit in his philosophy or world view are considerations about the individual and moral responsibility, the demands and imperfections of society, and the influence of nature and fate in a hostile world, themes which will receive attention in later chapters of this study.

A value which Aldecoa prized above all others in his work was authenticity. Although he wrote from experience, he held that "What matters first and foremost is truth."[37] A crucial distinction is thus asserted between factuality and verisimilitude, a distinction exemplified in *Great Sole*. This novel has consistently been interpreted as a documentary faithful in geographical and sociological detail to the experience of those Spanish sailors who fish in the area of Great Sole. Investigations carried out in Bantry Bay in the Southwest of Ireland nevertheless show that descriptions of people and places in chapter 7 of the book do not correspond to the actual circumstances of the town and surrounding area in the 1950s. Although Aldecoa sailed the fishing area of Great Sole and visited Bantry Bay in mid-summer of 1955, he did not resolve to slavishly record realistic detail of the voyage but rather to achieve a verisimilar literary recreation of that experience.

Those critics who have reduced Aldecoa's work to the level of verbal photography, ornate documentary, or literary sociology have overlooked his fundamental skill in "making something metaphorical out of reality."[38] For he would take his subject matter from often unexceptional sources and proceed to transform it poetically. This process of poetic transformation generally involves the interpretation of lived or observed experience and its suffusion with sensibility, and the structuring and motivated presentation of this subject matter with a view to the creation of an autonomous fictional whole. An intellectual with a firm critical appreciation of his métier, Aldecoa was faithful to artistic criteria. He objected to labels such as "the social novel," "the Catholic novel," or "the philosophical novel" in that their use prejudiced the integrity of the body of literature. "I look on novels purely as novels," he stated.[39] This does not mean that he subscribed to the belief in art for art's sake. As Julio Martínez de la Rosa has concluded, "Aldecoa [knew] that a novel is an end in itself, whose social value rests, above all, on the realization of its literary, artistic quality."[40]

A purist as regards the conception of his work, Aldecoa was equally scrupulous about its execution. Once he applied himself to the task of writing, "[his] sole concern [was] the well-finished work."[41] He had at his disposal a rich store of structural and narrative procedures which he would draw on and often modify in his search for the appropriate medium. "Although there are some denominators common to all an author's novels," he said, "each novel requires individual treatment and a mechanism and construction of its own."[42] Factors of technique, rhetoric, and style were, however, always instrumental to an overriding purpose identifiable as the archetypal goal of the writer of fiction, namely, to integrate the reader in an authentic fictional universe. Aldecoa summed up his essential ambition and expectations when he stated in a mature conversation: "What I want more than anything else is that whoever reads a book of mine should enter within the compass of the text. I subordinate virtually everything to this aim."[43] His success as a novelist may be gauged in the main by the extent to which he realized this essential goal.

IV   *The Short Story*

While the foregoing observations are valid as reflections on Aldecoa's work in general, they fall short of an adequate estimation of his principles as a writer of short stories and fiction of intermediate length. Many critics have indeed tended to confine their interest to his novels. The relative neglect of his stories is symptomatic of certain professional conditions and prejudices which prevailed in Spanish letters during the 1950s and 1960s. When Aldecoa declared in 1956 that "A novel is easier to place with a publisher than a volume of stories,"[44] he gave an accurate appraisal of the situation in its crudest commercial terms. Adelaide Burns and Erna Brandenberger may rightly celebrate the quality of stories written in Spain since the Civil War, particularly in the mid and late fifties, as indicating a renaissance of the genre,[45] but the difficulty of publication remained a constant obstacle during and beyond that period, as Ana María Matute confirmed in an article translated for the *Kenyon Review* in 1969.[46] Such a situation adversely affected attitudes to the short story. Medardo Fraile has documented the commentators' habit of dismissing the story as "a training ground for, or transition toward, the novel."[47] Aldecoa witnessed the same phenomenon and, like Fraile and the poet José Hierro,[48] mounted a vigorous defense of the short story as an independent genre.

The author's basic assumptions appear in miscellaneous declarations and, particularly, in his essay "The Modern Short Story in the U.S.A." Central to his poetics is the discrimination between writer ("escritor"), novelist ("novelista"), and storyteller ("narrador"). "I believe I am essentially a storyteller," he said,[49] thereby attributing to himself the qualities of the effective narrator before those of the fluent stylist or the imaginative creator and interpreter of human types and situations. The fact that his work provides both an inventory of stylistic procedures in a refined state of application, and a coherent body of significant characters, does not detract from this self-appraisal. Aldecoa was fond of citing the epitaph of Robert Louis Stevenson, and appropriated for himself the label "a teller of tales."

Aldecoa used the terms "cuento," "historia," "narración," and "relato" to identify his stories, but declined to differentiate substantially between them. While he dismissed terminological distinctions as "having absolutely nothing to do with the intrinsic value of the works concerned,"[50] he nevertheless appreciated the many forms a short story can take. In his essay he adverted significantly to the promitive legend and moral tale as two of the many possible variants. The distinctions he employed to define the particularity of the genre have their origin in considerations of form and technique. Aldecoa defended the "distinctive physiology," narrative proportions, and rhythm of the short story, where he believed the basic unit to be the word, not the event as in the conventional novel.[51] Such attention to the smallest functional element indicates a concern with economy which has traditionally been associated with the short story writer. From Edgar Allan Poe Aldecoa inherited the principle of the subordination of incident to a single effect and organic design, and he followed Guy de Maupassant in advocating an objective narrative mode as the most efficient means of eliciting the reflexive reader's collaboration. These precepts situate him squarely within a modern tradition of narrative.

Although in theory Aldecoa paid overwhelming attention to functional aspects of the short story, in practice he showed an unerring intuition of the elusive substance, or essential nature, of the genre. Bernard Bergonzi has put forward the two-fold view that "The [modern] short story deals with life's victims, the insulted and injured, the forlorn and alienated," and that "The modern short story writer is bound to see the world in a certain way, not merely because of our customary atmosphere of crisis, but because the form of the short story tends to filter down experience to the prime elements of defeat and alienation."[52] In many instances Aldecoa's work conforms to the type of the age defined here, for he took as his subject matter the working lives and everyday existence of humble people, focussing on social outcasts and life's victims in particular. But he was also successful in transcending the moral limitations of such a view. What he consistently aimed to do was to capture the depth and immediacy of human experience by exploiting the allusive and economical technique of the story. Accordingly, his short narratives evince a quality of sensibility, of sentiment fused with thought, to which the analytic and discursive technique of the novel would be inimical. They then assume poetic qualities which are substantially those imputed to the genre by Mariano Baquero Goyanes,[53] and bear out Adelaide Burns' claim that the short story by its nature provides "a condensed vision" of life.[54] For that succinct phrase conveys both the essence of Aldecoa's technique and the quality of sensibility distilled in his narratives.

V *Literary Influences*

The principal influences upon Aldecoa's work were Spanish and North American writers of prose and poetry from the classical and contemporary periods. A summary list such as that compiled by Ana María Navales would include the names of, on the one hand, Cervantes and Quevedo, Baroja, Azorín, and Valle-Inclán, the poets of the Generation of 1927, and Camilo José Cela, and on the other, Melville, Henry James, Hemingway, Faulkner, Steinbeck, and other members of the "lost generation." Aldecoa's debt to French literature must also be mentioned: Baudelaire and Verlaine, Maupassant, Proust, Saint Exupéry and Malraux, Simone de Beauvoir, Sartre and Camus all made an impact on him. English and German literature are represented but minimally on the shelves of his private library, the only figures of note being Conrad, Graham Greene, Kafka, Heine, and Thomas Mann. While these references may suggest an academic bias, it should be added that Aldecoa possessed some fifty detective novels by Simenon and a whole range of popular literature whose influence on him may not improperly be compared with that of the critical writings of Poe and Ortega y Gasset, or the Holy Bible.

The nature and extent of the influence of various authors upon Ignacio Aldecoa may perhaps be gauged by indicating analogies in precise aspects of his personality and work. As regards his temperament and attitude to his fellowman, he could find a reflection of his pessimism in the work of Dostoevski, Maupassant, Kafka, Faulkner, and particularly, Baroja. His instinctive vitalism was nevertheless corroborated by reading Jack London, Saint Exupéry (*Vol de nuit* and *Citadel*), and Hemingway, whose stories *The Old Man and the Sea,* "Fifty Grand," and "The Undefeated" excited Aldecoa's own passion for sea adventure, boxing, and bullfighting. He knew also Vicente Blasco Ibañez's *Sangre y arena* (*Blood and Sand*) and the three volumes of *La vuelta al mundo de un novelista* (*A Novelist's Trip Around the World*) by the same author. His own work in the travel genre continues the contemporary Spanish tradition of Azorín and Cela. The universal body of literature about the sea was also a potent source of inspiration to him. Among the list of authors whose work he assessed in his essay "A Sea of Tales" are the following: Stevenson, Defoe, Verne, Salgari, Wyss, Fenimore Cooper, Melville, Conrad, and among Spaniards, Alvar Núñez Cabeza de Vaca and Baroja. Finally, Aldecoa's outlook on his fellowman is imbued with the humanitarian spirit of Camus, whose work he admired, Faulkner, whose speech upon accepting the Nobel Prize for 1949 he cited, and Steinbeck, whose work exhibits a profound sense of social justice and human sympathy identical to his own.

The predominant social themes of the "lost generation" are echoed in Aldecoa's writing: the decadence of a social jet set, exposed by Scott Fitzgerald and Dos Passos; the rebellion of the outsider, exemplified by Kerouac; the exploitation of the unprotected, as indicated by Steinbeck. Eugenio de Nora also suggests the influence of Richard Wright, author of *Native Son*. Spanish sources for the same themes and preoccupations include Larra, Galdós, Baroja, and Valle-Inclán, to whose *Sonatas* an .oblique reference is made in section 6 of Aldecoa's story "Ave del Paraíso" ("Bird of Paradise").

For several years, when accounting for the influences on Aldecoa's work, critics confined their attention to aspects of content. The balance has since been redressed by others who have sought to identify the origin of the author's technical principles. Fernando Arrojo, for example, points to Henry James and Maupassant, authors with whose work Aldecoa was certainly familiar, as he was with that of Flaubert and Faulkner. In his fastidious reappraisal of conventions, he may rightly be considered heir to those writers who posited the novel and short story to be problematical art forms and contributed to the development of a modern poetics of fiction.

Aldecoa's use of myth and archetype, and his cultivation of the fable are areas of technique in which it is possible to discern the influences of Melville, Faulkner, and Steinbeck. The epic resonances and moral inquiry of *Great Sole* may be traced to *Moby Dick*. Faulkner's novel *A Fable*, the subject of a long review in *Cuadernos Hispanoamericanos* for March 1955, is another source of allegorical design, as are Steinbeck's *The Grapes of Wrath* and *East of Eden*, which together provide the basis of Aldecoa's story "Solar del paraíso" ("Paradise Lot").

Certain literary movements and styles left their mark on Aldecoa's writing. José Ramón Marra López and José Luis Cano have underlined his debt to the Spanish tradition of metaphor and conceit represented by Quevedo, Valle-Inclán, and Ramón Gómez de la Serna. He possessed copies of *Los sueños* (*The Dreams*) by Quevedo, and *Flor de greguerías* — translatable as *A Bouquet of Conceits* — and other books by Gómez de la Serna. Cervantes, Baroja, and Azorín are among the sources of his major styles: the ironic, laconic, and lyrical.

As far as the short novel and story are concerned, Aldecoa acknowledged *The Old Man and the Sea* by Hemingway, *Death in Venice* by Thomas Mann, and "Boule de Suif" by Maupassant, as representing the highest standards attainable in fiction. Maupassant and Hemingway's perceptive exploration, in a spare narrative form, of hidden aspects of everyday life provided Aldecoa with examples from which to work. As remarked in a previous section, he was also significantly influenced by Poe in his conception of the short story.

Lastly, Aldecoa's work in the medium of poetry is by his own admission a labor of imitation. He took as his principal models of sensibility and expression Góngora and Saint John of the Cross, pastoral poetry from Virgil to the Basque Ramón de Basterra, Verlaine, Antonio Machado and Juan Ramón Jiménez, Rafael Alberti and Vicente Aleixandre, Miguel Hernández and the *garcilasistas,* and Carlos Edmundo de Ory. This range of references adequately illustrates the scope of Aldecoa's literary interests and his spirit of eclecticism.

CHAPTER 3

The First Novel:
El fulgor y la sangre

I *Aspects of Content*

ALDECOA defined the starting point of his novels in an interview with Miguel Fernández Braso held in 1968: "I take a
situation ... and exhaust its possibilities.... I choose something
which places a limit on the characters' lives, something which is
consequently more dramatic than their everyday experience. This
hermetic and predetermined tragic setting is what interests me."[1] *El
fulgor y la sangre* (*Blood and Lightning*) is a practical illustration
of this method. The plot revolves upon an arbitrary event which
precipitates a crisis in a limited setting. An unidentified civil guard
has been seriously wounded, and possibly killed, while on patrol
with three of his colleagues. At the local headquarters, an inhospitable castle starkly set apart from a north Castilian villiage, the first
to be informed of the accident, shortly after midday, are Regino
Ruipérez and Pedro Sánchez, the guard and sentry on duty. The
narrative then gradually traces the reactions of five women, Sonsoles, Felisa, María, Carmen, and Ernesta, as they learn that one of
the men in their close community is perhaps dead. The collective
anxiety and sinister expectations of more than seven hours are
eventually dispelled when the patrol returns at nightfall, bearing
the corpse of the corporal Francisco Santos, a bachelor, who was
killed that noon by a Gypsy, following a disturbance at a local fair.

Both José Corrales Egea and Santos Sanz Villanueva have ques-
tioned the very foundation of this "predetermined tragic setting,"
arguing that the profession of civil guard is intrinsically dangerous
and that threats to a guard's life have nothing to do with fate.[2] But
it is the woman's tragic experience which is the subject of *Blood
and Lightning*. The fatality of the situation described in the novel

rests on the fact that they are victims of their husbands' decisions and are not directly responsible for their involvement in a fortuitous drama.

This boundary- or test-situation holds many "possibilities" for the novelist. Aldecoa concentrates on three essentials: he explores the characters' psychology; he analyzes the thematic and philosophical implications of the situation; and he exploits its narrative potential for drama, suspense, and irony. He penetrates the mind of his characters and traces "the threads of distress forming a web throughout the castle."[3] In the long period of enforced waiting, the wives and colleagues of the men on patrol give free rein to their impulsive emotions and imagination as a substitute for physical activity. Pedro fills "the emptiness of guard duty" (8) with wide-ranging thoughts about his family responsibilities and inescapable professional obligations; Felisa, bewildered by the apparent ease with which a human life can be lost, feels the pervasive and almost palpable presence of misfortune in the castle; the obsession of securing a transfer to another civil guard headquarters is a common distraction from the reigning disquietude. *Blood and Lightning* is a disturbing investigation of human reactions under stress, and a model for Aldecoa's subsequent novels.

The inhabitants' anguished sense of impotence and alienation in a setting which resembles a prison or "a strange purgatory of boredom, despair and habit" (11) provides some justification for Pablo Borau's interpretation of *Blood and Lightning* as an existentialist novel.[4] Echoes of Kafka (*The Castle*) and Sartre (*Huis Clos*) are present throughout and are sounded in Aldecoa's own declaration that the characters of *Blood and Lightning* "are not waiting simply to discover who the dead man is but, more important, to escape from a perpetually sealed world, a world without horizons...."[5] The ideas of the monotonous foundation of everyday life and its gratuitous interruption by an absurd event may well be Camusian; and the "predetermined tragic setting" may be traced to Heidegger's theory of the *Grenz-situation* (border line situation). But an inflexible classification of Aldecoa's novels as "existentialist" runs the risk of detracting from the particularity, and very Spanish quality, of his reflections on human nature and destiny, which are at the most symptomatic of a general philosophical atmosphere and are perforce independent of any specific movement. Aldecoa's view of the world and humanity as it is expressed here recalls Pío Baroja's somber attitude. Man is the victim of

external forces: fate, nature, political and social constraints. He is
pitched into a grim struggle for survival, without the hope of salvation or the solace of assistance from his fellowman. His life is
devoid of purpose, a condition of endless "waiting" ("espera") for
unlikely solution. The title of a volume of stories published in 1955
Espera de tercera clase (*Waiting Room, Third Class*), reiterates
Aldecoa's pessimistic conception of human existence.

Aldecoa expresses important historical themes in *Blood and
Lightning*. The guards and their wives all share a common social
and political heritage specified in frequent references to crucial
dates and events of the period between 1920 and 1950. The dominant factor in their lives has been the Spanish Civil War of
1936–1939. Retrospective sections of the narrative which alternate
with the main sequence of events tell the life stories of all the
characters apart from the corporal, who provides a potted auto-
biography while conversing with his colleague Arenas. Excepting
the youthful Guillermo and Ernesta, all have experienced the Civil
War as sensitive adolescents or adults: María's date of birth is estimated to be 1915, while the text shows that the corporal was born
in 1920, Carmen in 1922, and Sonsoles in 1923. Through a variety
of characters Aldecoa surveys life in Castile during a period of
some forty years. Of the five women portrayed in detail, all but one
have working-class origins, with María coming from a middle-class
family. Sonsoles and Ernesta were brought up in a poor agricultural environment, Felisa comes from a provincial town where her
father was at one time employed on the railway, and Carmen has
spent the first twenty to twenty-five years of her life in Madrid,
where her father worked as a craftsman in metal.

The prevailing political ideology in these households was left-
wing, the most extreme manifestation being commitment to the
proletarian revolution, as in the case of Felisa's brother. Aldecoa
analyzes the complex effects of political involvement on this family
with sympathetic insight. Juan, the father, was too easily maneu-
vered into a dangerous position of open support for the Republican
cause, and as a result was detained and imprisoned at the outbreak
of the war. Intervention on his behalf by Felisa's fiancé, Ruipérez,
secures Juan's eventual release, after which he manages to find a
job for a short time in a Nationalist arms factory, making bomb
fuses. By a cruel irony of circumstance, he is actually contributing
to the fight against the Republican cause which his own son is
defending. Sensitive, no doubt, to the constraints of censorship,

Aldecoa shows his understanding and tacit support for those who like Juan Martín were victims of political accident, and for the poor and underprivileged Spaniards who were subject to the abuses of landowners, moneylenders, the police, and other reactionary elements.

In appreciation of these historical themes, Eugenio de Nora aptly describes *Blood and Lightning* as "a probing into the collective consciousness of postwar Spain."[6] It certainly qualifies as an example of that critical costumbrism and historical realism which Castellet and Curutchet regard as the prominent mode of Spanish fiction in the 1950s.[7]

II   *Aspects of Technique and Style*

In his first novel Aldecoa sets out to exploit the dramatic potential of human behavior under artificial circumstances, and fabricates a powerful and engaging narrative. The opening paragraph of the first chapter establishes an atmosphere of boredom and immobility, rendered complex by a suggestion that danger is imminent. Pedro's reflections on the ever-present threat of an outbreak of hysteria inside the living quarters are a calculated preface to the telephone call which announces that a guard has been shot. Nervousness and a sense of impotence permeate the conclusion of chapter 1 in a fertile combination which enriches the remaining three hundred and twenty-two pages of the novel.

The text of *Blood and Lightning* is divided into temporal segments instead of conventional chapters, and headings are replaced by references to the clock. Narrative rhythm is all-important and is founded for the most part on the careful distribution of scenes in which the disquieting news is revealed to the characters at selected intervals. The guard on duty learns at midday, in a scene described on page 14. Sonsoles finds out at one minute past two, on page 57, and Ruipérez tells Felisa just before three o'clock, on page 103. Sonsoles and Felisa together inform María shortly before half-past four, on page 184, and she breaks the news to Carmen at about half-past five, on page 245. Ernesta, the youngest and most impressionable of the group finds out immediately thereafter, on page 246. Finally, María tells her son, the oldest of the children in the castle, at seven o'clock, on page 321. Once all the women have been informed, dramatic tension is maintained by Ernesta's periodic nervous crises. The suspense becomes more acute as the time

approaches for the patrol to return. The women at last discover the
dead man's identity in a scene of explosive relief described on page
340, two pages before the end of the novel. The narrative thus consists of a sustained emotional crescendo, moving toward a denoue-
ment which is purposively prepared.

The building up of a storm reflects metaphorically the rhythm of
human expectations carefully plotted throughout. In the stifling
midday heat Pedro compares human frenzy to "a dry storm in the
sultry atmosphere" (13), and shortly after tells his wife that "[he]
would not be at all surprised if there was a storm gathering" (33).
As the characters' anxiety intensifies, the afternoon heat becomes
more oppressive, until Ruipérez the guard feels "the storm
threatening to break" (224–25). With the disclosure that it is the
corporal who has been killed, there comes a relieving of tension,
mirrored in the storm's breaking some distance from the castle:
"The air was still heavy. It would freshen immediately" (341).

The pattern of balanced linear development is complemented by
the structural arrangement of retrospective fragments, an example
of Aldecoa's technical debt to William Faulkner. Each of the five
central chapters tells the life-story of a woman character, in
chronological but interrupted sequence. This secondary narrative
has an eventful and dynamic quality, compensating for the lack of
action in the primary plot and providing important variety for the
reader. But the author also uses retrospective material to vary the
rhythm of the story line, inserting it in increasing proportions
throughout the text. In the chapter entitled "Two in the afternoon" slightly less than fifty percent of the narrative refers to Sonsoles' past. "Half past four in the afternoon" comprises no less
than sixty-five percent devoted to María's past. In the penultimate
chapter the proportion has now increased to seventy-three percent
versus twenty-seven percent, a compositional procedure aimed at
retarding the imminent revelation of the dead guard's identity.

The narrative acquires additional aesthetic shape from the hermetic framework in which it is set. *Blood and Lightning* opens with
the news that a man has been wounded; the concluding chapter
contains a substantial retrospective section which reports the circumstances of that morning's accident. This cyclical pattern
emphasizes the dramatic compression of space, time, and action in
the novel, and gives formal expression to the prevailing mood of
menacing claustrophobia: "Vulnerability, unrest and fear are three
concentric circles, in the minds of the women at the castle, within

which silence unfolds..." (290). The final paragraph releases tension by suddenly transferring perspective to the countryside beyond the castle, where a frightened figure responsible for Santos' death is on the run.

Aldecoa accords the same careful attention to narrative method and style as to structural composition. Use of poetic motifs, binary opposition, foreshadowing, and a rigorous control of the narrative temper produce a cohesive work. Motifs borrowed from the world of nature are prominent throughout *Blood and Lightning*. The novel opens with a scene in which Pedro destroys an ant trail: "Then, quite bored, he would look at the mournful and perfect organization of the insects, until they recovered the normality and urgency of routine" (7). This image adumbrates the disruption of human routine portrayed in the plot. Subsequent passages indirectly compare defenseless human beings with flies "striving to escape" and "driven mad by the heat" (180–81). Animals have the same representative function. While Francisco Santos is dying in the nearby countryside, children in the castle torment a toad they have managed to catch, ironically shouting for some water to revive it. Water too is a symbolic motif, aptly complementing the omnipresent references to heat and sun. Ernesta wishes there were a river near the castle, and Pedro would give anything for a refreshing glass of water with vinegar and sugar, as he stands on guard. The novel's title is also charged with symbolic value. Both narrator and characters describe, recall, or imagine bloody scenes, insistently emphasizing the physical threat to human life. Ruipérez envisages the moment of death as "a flash which would be the first stage of never seeing again" (74). This body of motifs indicates the hostility of nature and the environment to human life.

Contrasts between certain images, ideas, situations, or characters also enhance the narrative's substance and depth. The motifs of heat-water and light-shade are complementary pairs; the variation of scenes relating to the characters' past and present, and to events happening inside and outside the castle, underlines the opposition between reality and imagination, imprisonment and freedom, and the conflicting moods of anxiety and relief. María's strong but perverse nature is offset strikingly against Ernesta's candor and vulnerability. A fruitful and ironic contrast is drawn between responsible adult life and innocent childhood play. War games offer a shocking parallel with the civil disturbance of 1936–1939, and there is a literally vital difference between a child's attitude to make-believe and the real professional duties of an armed civil guard.

Aldecoa obliquely prepares the reader for the outcome of the plot by distinguishing the corporal from the other guards. He is the only bachelor in the group; the narrator gives no retrospective account of his life; and at six o'clock a telegram arrives, singling him out for transfer to another position. There are also obtuse hints that the corporal might be the dead guard. Felisa regards him as stubborn, and fears for the safety of the men in his patrol. And María secretly hopes that he is the victim, because a bachelor's death does not affect the happiness and welfare of a dependent family. The eventual outcome in fact confirms the women's premonitions and the reader's carefully aroused suspicion. Upon the novel's publication José María Castellet expressed reservations about the dramatic effectiveness of this conclusion, which may appear bathetic and contrived to those with ungenerous expectations.[8] However, Gustavo Pérez Firmat has correctly related the mechanism of narrative suspense to the preparation of an ironic solution,[9] which is at the root of Aldecoa's art here. The text of *Blood and Lightning* is riddled with instances of irony. The narrator's unobtrusive comment that Ruipérez was originally posted to the castle as a replacement for a dead colleague points to a coincidence which will not escape the attentive reader. There is also perverse but compelling humor in an ambivalent remark made by María's mother, that "Every child has a Guardian Angel as big as a castle" (158). Such ambiguous comments have a potent effect on the reader's sensibility, challenging his expectations as to how the plot may conclude. Juan Luis Alborg was among the first critics to praise the ambiguous and restrained narrative temper of *Blood and Lightning,*[10] which serves ultimately to highlight the awesome predictability of fate.

Aldecoa uses two styles in the novel. One is sober, economical, and clear, in the manner of Hemingway and Baroja, and is used, for the main part, in dialogue, objective description, and the presentation of dramatic material. The other is evocative, dense, and complex, at times languid and sensuous, reminiscent of Azorín; it is used in psychological analysis and the description of nature. The two styles contrast or combine according to context.

The opening three paragraphs exhibit the rich texture of Aldecoa's prose. Typical semantic features include: vocabulary related to the senses, which shows Aldecoa's acute physical awareness and psychological sensitivity; exhaustive pursuit of detail; plastic imagery which may graduate to simile and metaphor, as in the description "la bandada de grajos, negros y tormentosos" ("the flock of crows, black and stormy"); and the synthesis of disparate qualities, as in the phrase "la triste y perfecta organización de los insectos" ("the insects' mournful and perfect organization"). Characteristic of the syntax are: occasional anaphora; conjunction of adjectives, nouns, or phrases in groups of three; and complex and symmetrical combination of clauses. Such writing produces an effect of density quite in keeping with the atmosphere of tedium and distraction cultivated in the novel.

The dramatic sequence reprinted below relates the brutal death of Sonsoles' father at the beginning of the war, and illustrates the complementary style of sinuous restraint:

De unas ruinas asomaron los cañones de una escopeta de caza. Los campesinos avanzaron más. Se oyó un grito terrible. Sacaron a un hombre con los pantalones chorreando sangre. Alguien se acercó con la navaja abierta y le dió un tajo en la boca. El labio inferior le quedó colgando. El hombre escupió un borbotón de sangre. Dijo algo que no se le entendió. Lo remataron a puñaladas y se alejaron. (19)

Shotgun barrels poked out from inside some ruins. The peasants walked on ahead. A terrible cry rang out. They dragged out a man with blood dripping from his trousers. Some one went up to him with a razor and slashed him in the mouth. His lower lip flopped down. The man spat out a gob of blood. He said something no one understood. They stabbed him to death and went away.

The rapid, staccato sequence of no less than twelve verbs in the preterite tense, the economy of clauses, paucity of adjectives, and simplicity of vocabulary produce an appropriate graphic effect. Aldecoa's sensitivity to language, whether written or spoken, popular or refined, is evident in *Blood and Lightning*.

The various aspects of technique enumerated here are glossed in certain passages of interior duplication. Aldecoa analyzes with critical detachment the aesthetic elements and conventions employed in the text. Most of the characters in *Blood and Lightning* have recourse to telling stories which vary in content, manner, and purpose. The "serene" tales which Felisa used to tell her brothers and sisters during the war contrast vividly with the dramatic evocation of suffering and hardship in which the village priest, Carmen, and María take delight. María's is a particularly

interesting case. Her penchant for violent, crude, and exciting tales
was fostered by talkative people like her father and the woman with
whom she lodged while teaching in a mountain village before the
war. Literature reserved for the adult members of her family was an
irresistible temptation to her as an adolescent, and exerted a further
influence on her. The cultivated horror and vulgarity of María's
tremendist stories are qualities which do not appeal to everybody.
Felisa complains that "We all know life has its seamy side, but
there are wholesome and attractive things which she never mentions" (106), a remark which shows Aldecoa's reservations about
tremendism.

    These reflexive passages present a probing inquiry into problems
of narrative presentation. Characters distort and elaborate details
of their own and other people's experience, or sometimes invent an
imaginary alternative. Legend or myth may eventually result from
such variations. A ready technical device is the manipulation of
narrative tempo. Sonsoles is aware of its potential flexibility:
"There was no constant measure of time. Events marked time. . . .
Whole years could be accounted for in just one moment" (86). The
way in which María treats time is crucial to the effect her stories
have on the naive, impressionable Ernesta. The importance of style
is also recognized. Although the subject matter of Carmen's narrative is often unpleasant, her manner is lyrical, evoking a general
response of "sweet nostalgia." On the other hand, "when María
told a story about a crime, a brutal adultery, or primitive passions,
even though they were imaginary, it was as if everything she
described was real: the darkness would appear to thicken, sins
acquire the same compelling force they have in the Bible, or the
crime turn into a great pool of blood washing over the feet of the
people listening to her" (178). Finally, stories are said to serve
various purposes. They cater for the imaginative needs of a person
like Carmen, who finds no inspiration in life at the castle, and they
satisfy María's perverse desire to corrupt and frighten Ernesta. In
context, stories help to distract attention from the grimness of reality, filling the empty hours of morbid silence. Once Sonsoles has
learned the shattering news, she perceives the use to which storytelling may be put, as a means of concealing truth. She fabricates a
narrative in which the attentive María nevertheless detects an unut-
tered confession.

    The majority of these comments on the art of storytelling have
direct bearing on the text of *Blood and Lightning.* Those which

treat of the suitability of violent topics, the cultivation of a mood of mystery and suspense, and the role of time in narrative technique offer apposite and valuable information as to how the novel is to be appreciated. Felisa's recognition that "There were times when the whole affair seemed like an old story she had recently heard, something frightening which had actually happened, but which had nothing to do with their quiet life in the castle" (151) encourages the reader to identify with the crisis described in the story by affirming the authenticity of imagined experience. In the fifth chapter of *Blood and Lightning,* Aldecoa again anticipates and influences the reader's response to the contrived drama in the novel. There is a crucial implication in the fact that María's imaginary version of what could have happened to the guards on patrol corresponds with uncanny exactness to the narrator's version. María's story actually "hypnotizes" Sonsoles, a poetic effect which we may assume to be analogous with the impression that a reading of *Blood and Lightning* may produce.

Gustavo Pérez Firmat suggests that here Aldecoa was indulging in "the game of exposing the conventions of fiction."[11] Aldecoa was indeed criticized for pursuing excessively technical goals in his early work, and the charge of virtuosity may still be sustained against him in this instance, on the basis of the occasionally gratuitous interior duplication and the schematic, predictable pattern of the narrative which one critic regards as so artificial as to be a "parody of itself."[12] Such technical virtuosity may be judged to have prevented Aldecoa from exploiting to the full the thematic "possibilities" of his material. However, *Blood and Lightning* possesses a thematic richness absent from the majority of Spanish novels of the period. It is also a work of narrative verve, discerning characterization, and accomplished style. In this his first novel Aldecoa was engaged in the bold reappraisal of established conventions regarding subject matter, plot, technique, and style. Melchor Fernández Almagro confidently adjudged the appearance of *Blood and Lightning* "a very happy event in the literary world."[13] Runner-up in the competition for the Planeta Prize in 1954, the book is both a promising individual effort and a valuable contribution to the work of an emerging generation.

CHAPTER 4

The Second Novel:
Con el viento solano

I   *Analysis of Plot*

*C*on *el viento solano* (*With the East Wind*) is a companion volume to *Blood and Lightning*. It complements and extends the
narrative of that novel by describing the episode and consequences
of Francisco Santos' death from the point of view of his murderer,
a Gypsy delinquent named Sebastián Vázquez. The action covers a
period of six days in late July, each of which is treated in a separate
chapter. Chapter 1 opens with some scenes of the red-light area in
Talavera where Sebastián is drinking into the small hours of Monday morning. In the first tableau an atmosphere of vulgarity and
decay is suggested by a seedy picture hanging on a dirty wall, and a
clock which has stopped. Sebastián makes a dramatic entry, speaking gruffly to a female brothel owner. Among his companions in
these scenes are Lupe, the woman he exploits, and Larios, a fellow
Gypsy and petty criminal. Soon after daybreak he and Larios leave
Talavera for a neighboring village where a fair is in progress. Under
the continuing influence of drink, they stir up trouble at a stall and
the arrogant Sebastián attacks el Maño, the owner, with a broken
glass. He then runs away across open country with Francisco
Santos, the *guardia,* in pursuit. When finally cornered and ordered
to surrender, Sebastián answers the corporal's challenge by shooting him. From this point on he is a confused and frightened fugitive
from justice.

The narrative in the five remaining chapters follows Sebastián's
declining fortunes as he looks in vain for shelter and support from
friends and relatives in Campamento, Madrid, Alcalá, and Cogolludo. On Tuesday he takes a train to Campamento, on the outskirts
of Madrid, and asks for help from a friend, Francisco Vázquez,

54

who is reluctant to become involved with a wanted man. So Sebastián goes on to Madrid where he spends some time with a maudlin prostitute, Pepita, before retiring to cheap lodgings for the night. The next casual acquaintance he makes, upon awaking on Wednesday morning, is José Cabeda, a philosophical ex-convict, who aggravates Sebastián's anxiety by informing him that Francisco Santos actually died in the shooting. Afraid of remaining in one place too long, Sebastián leaves Madrid and travels to Alcalá, where he spends much of Thursday. In Alcalá his uncle refuses him either protection or the minimum of hospitality, and he is obliged to move on to Cogolludo, where his mother lives. On Friday afternoon he tells her what he has done and begs for help, but she turns him away. His despair and disorientation are thus complete and he gives himself up to the police the following night.

Beyond certain coincidences and similarities in setting and plot, *With the East Wind* shares with *Blood and Lightning* a penetrating analysis of human behavior under extraordinary pressure. The various case histories found in the first novel are here replaced by the extended examination of an individual's psychological development. At the outset, with his tiresome boastful manner, Sebastián conforms to the stereotype of the Spanish *chulo*. But following the attack on el Maño, instinctive feelings of fear and insecurity take hold of him, assuming the force of panic and anguish after he has shot Francisco Santos. He is obliged to take stock of his position and to recognize, beneath the layers of social pretence and habit, fundamental and sobering truths about himself. The reunion with Francisco Vázquez is important in this respect, since it produces a quite unprecedented degree of critical self-awareness in Sebastián. He sees how his life has been inauthentic up to this moment, and motivated by fear, laziness, and unthinking instinct. His brief encounter with Casimiro, an unfortunate idiot who sings and dances in a bar at Alcalá, is a similar incident, serving to reveal to him the way his life is gradually losing all value. At the end his surrender to the authorities implies an admission of impotence and spiritual bankruptcy for which there is no remedy.

Sebastián develops in many other ways. He acquires a profound sense of the value of freedom, and a keen perception of his relation to others. He forfeits his legal freedom as a citizen when he shoots the civil guard, but subsequently realizes that he has lost a more essential type of freedom which he recognizes in Roque the fakir and Casimiro *el bobo:* that is, the ontological freedom of an individual, however materially poor or physically disabled, to act according to the dictates of his conscience. With regard to his social relations, Sebastián moves from a position of dominance to one of dependence. He takes other people for granted before the crime, but soon regrets being a liability to an innocent friend like Francisco Vázquez or his uncle's family. These changes are reflected in his attitude to Lupe. The complacency and cruelty typical of a *chulo* give way to a sincere sense of loss which Sebastián experiences upon entering Cogolludo, for example. Although for a time he fabricates a naive image of his relationship with Lupe, he arrives at a coldly realistic view, and admits, in a passage of direct interior monologue, that even if he were able to return to her, he would inevitably mistreat and abuse her: "But I am not to return to Talavera. It is too late. There's nothing to be done. I'd only carry on harming the only thing worth returning for. No, Lupe is now no more than a memory; she must be only a memory in order that everything run its course."[1]

Through the acquisition of such insights Sebastián comes to feel increasingly alienated from the world about him. While waiting for the train to take him to Madrid, he imagines himself to be a lone soldier caught in no man's land on a battle field. The experience of alienation is doubly severe at Alcalá, because he is both aware of his social incompatibility and a witness to the disintegration of his personality, in which the ideal harmony of thought and feeling has been shattered: "Sebastián, or his mind, was floundering in this sea of activity. He was possibly the only part out of place, an elusive loose end which was not absorbed by the massive energy of the fair" (184).

Memory has an important role to play in Sebastián's psychology. It affords a natural distraction from the dilemmas and obsessions assailing him. The casual recollection of childhood scenes consoles him as he travels toward Madrid, but he soon sees the limitations and dangers of solitary retrospection. In Cogolludo he feels the urgent need "to taste the sweetness of communal memories" with members of his family (234), as a means of recovering the ideal security of time past. But the connection is severed when his mother rejects him and, in keeping with his overall psychological decline, the process of Sebastián's memory degenerates into an arbitrary mechanism in which intelligence plays no part.

II *Aspects of Content*

Of all Aldecoa's novels, *With the East Wind* has generated most serious critical interest. The various interpretations of Sebastián Vázquez's experience fall into two major categories: the social and the existential, thereby reflecting that polarity of opinion which informs much discussion of the contemporary Spanish novel. In this particular instance, however, a tendency to dogmatism has threatened to obscure the variety of themes in the book, as the exponents of one view have paid insufficient attention to elements or features which support another. A comprehensive and balanced appraisal is therefore not only desirable but would also correspond to the author's own intentions more faithfully than existing approaches. Aldecoa hoped "to bring out the contrast between the anguish of a man on the run and the indifference of the world about him," for, as he added, "Nothing matters to the world in general, anguish is always strictly personal."[2] He accordingly shows the interplay of social and ontological factors in Sebastián's experience, and points to conclusions which have significance on a wide plane.

As a document of social reality, *With the East Wind* examines the position of an underprivileged group, the Gypsies. Aldecoa sketches a picture of their hermetic community and marginal status. Their mores and language give them a cultural identity which society at large does not trust or comprehend. They are particularly susceptible as regards the law, since their economic deprivation leads to inevitable forms of delinquency. Sebastián is a product of this unenviable environment. He grew up in an atmosphere of hardship and violence, subject to criminal influences, like his namesake in an earlier story, "The Humble Life of Sebastián Zafra." He is now particularly conscious of his position as an outsider, regarding himself as one of "los del camino" ("the people on the move"), whose misfortune it is to be systematically denied security and stability. He is in sympathy with those who, like José Cabeda and Pepita, are "outside the law" and "against society." After shooting the corporal, Sebastián suffers nothing less than a persecution complex, imagining that the entire Spanish police force will be mercilessly tracking him down. He fears punishment less than "the ritual of justice" (54), because the established code of justice is alien to him and his people.

While comparing *With the East Wind* with Richard Wright's abrasive novel about the American Negro, *Native Son,* Eugenio de

Nora complains that Aldecoa does not openly discuss the matter of the Gypsies' minority status or develop at length the question of environmental conditioning.[3] True, it lacks these controversial elements of sociological analysis, but the book is nevertheless a powerful account of human suffering in the context of society. Rafael Bosch has called *With the East Wind* "one of the best social novels of this period."[4] Gonzalo Sobejano describes it as "the realistic novel of Gypsy life," and quite rightly indicates that "In spite of his alcoholic fury, Sebastián Vázquez seems more of a victim than a delinquent."[5]

The idea of the victim is prominent throughout Aldecoa's work. In this instance it is significant in both a social and existential context. Sebastián is the victim of minority status in Spanish society, but he is also conditioned by metaphysical factors, as is indicated by the emphasis given in the novel to the themes of freedom, the influence of fate, and the role of chance and accidents in human life. A comparison with Camus' *L'Etranger* (*The Outsider*), hinted at by Janet Winecoff Díaz,[6] may shed some light on this aspect of the book, as Sebastián resembles Camus' Outsider in certain respects. His crime, like Meursault's, is in part the result of chance: the gun he uses to shoot Francisco Santos came into his possession "by chance." Like Meursault when he confronts the Arab on the beach, Sebastián commits murder under the momentary influence of forces beyond the pale of human reason: it is something instinctive and absurd which makes him pick up the gun "without realizing" and "mechanically" pull the trigger. A subsequent definition of crime as "no more than an accident at the animal level of life" (103) is inspired by the need to preserve an illusion of freedom in a hazardous world. For Sebastián ultimately decides that there is nothing he can do to prevent fate from running its destructive course.

Gemma Roberts, who has interpreted *With the East Wind* in the terms of reference of European existentialism, argues that the dominant theme of the novel is that of decision.[7] In her opinion, the narrative describes various stages of an existential conversion to authenticity, culminating in Sebastián's supposed decision to surrender to the civil guard. Such a view implies a very curious notion of human freedom and resolve, however, for *With the East Wind* portrays a man who, unlike the ideal existentialist hero, is manifestly unable to take decisions whereby to determine the course of his destiny. The following description of Sebastián at the Alcalá fair bears witness to his bewilderment, lack of willpower, and incapacity for action:

In that act of concentration — where memory made a plaintive sound — Sebastián was trying desperately to find himself. This desperation, this desire to find himself caused him anxiety — founded on his fear of objects and other people; founded on his inability to penetrate the consoling depths of memory; founded on his aimless course or flight — the boundless anxiety of loneliness. He could not think. He was just aware of one sensation. Sebastián sensed the presence of death in his life. (184)

If, as Aldecoa stated elsewhere, the agony of the human condition rests on the fact that "Fatality looms over man and man is free to accept or reject it,"[8] then Sebastián suffers on two accounts: as a pawn of fate, and as a victim of his own inability to take advantage of that quite notional freedom.

With the East Wind possesses a symbolic framework which enhances these social and existential themes, and points to their possible synthesis. Founded on material drawn from biblical sources, this system of symbolic references relates Sebastián's experience to certain archetypal situations and patterns of behavior. Bearing in mind Aldecoa's agnosticism and his patently secular view of the world, it may be assumed that his purpose in drawing parallels from Christian mythology is not didactic or doctrinal, as Charles Carlisle has inferred, but illustrative. Carlisle has evidenced Aldecoa's use of the image of the east wind, taken from the books of Amos and Haggai in the Old Testament. He regards the east wind as an agent of divine punishment, and dogmatically contends that "The most important aspect of Sebastián's alienation [is] his alienation from God." It is doubtful whether Aldecoa would have agreed with this, or that he accorded much significance to the fact that "Sebastián never turns to God for help in any manner, either through personal supplication or through the institution of the church."[9] In this instance the east wind is an instrument of adverse fate, and not of divine retribution enacted on an erring individual.

Pablo Borau has detected unmistakable echoes of Christian lore in, among other things, Sebastián's escape along the Via Crucis to an olive grove (40–42), and the conventional association of certain saints with five out of six days covered by the action.[10] The name of Mary Magdalene is ascribed to the first chapter, set on a Monday: by the terms of this analogy, Lupe is a sinner woman in the biblical tradition. The title of the fifth chapter, which relates the events of Friday when Sebastián's mother turns him away, refers with ironic incongruity to Anne, the patron saint of home and family life.

In addition, as Gonzalo Sobejano has suggested in an undeveloped aperçu,[11] Lupe may be seen as an Eve-like figure whose advice Sebastián ignores at the beginning of the book. Although Sebastián's relations with Lupe do not mirror exactly those between Adam and Eve, his suffering and nostalgia after the shooting are a clear instance of a fall from grace or emergence from paradise, albeit one of routine and ignorance. One of the characters whom Sebastián meets on his journey through Castile articulates this idea. José Cabeda, whom Borau sees as a good Samaritan figure, professes, in accordance with Christian teaching, that man has awakened from a perfect sleep into a world of implacable misfortune: "I have always believed that Paradise was nothing else than a good long sleep. Woman woke up Adam and he lost the power to sleep" (126). These words, spoken as the two men breakfast in Madrid, ring true to Sebastián who intuits a reflection of his own situation in Cabeda's fatalistic philosophy.

Within the context of biblical analogies, Sebastián's own name is also evocative of martyrdom. There is no textual evidence to identify him specifically with Saint Sebastian, but he is nevertheless suggestively likened unto the archetypal victims of persecution, the martyred saints. Again it is one of his wayfaring acquaintances who indicates the analogy. Roque, a Christian mystic obsessed with the lives of saints, tells Sebastián of one holy man who traveled widely and died a martyr. Sebastián is again deeply impressed by the oracular implications of the conversation, described on page 213. Though evidently no saint in his moral conduct or belief, he is a wanderer whose suffering assumes proportions of martyrdom. Denied by his own family, and reduced to a state of resignation so that he eventually gives himself up, Sebastián appears ultimately as a sacrificial victim.

In general, a martyr's behavior can only be comprehended fully in relation to a cause or group he represents. The group Sebastián represents in *With the East Wind* is that of the Gypsies in Spain. In fact, he is the unconscious expiator of their faults and offenses against the status quo. Outlawed by society and persecuted by the winds of fate, he symbolizes the Gypsy community which is denied access to any kind of paradise and destined to misfortune. James Abbott has commented on the theme of the journey to paradise in

Aldecoa's work;[12] in *With the East Wind* Aldecoa uses this and other biblical allusions to transform general considerations about society and human existence into a powerful protest on behalf of a minority group in Spain.

III   *Aspects of Technique*

From the point of view of construction and narrative technique, *With the East Wind* again resembles *Blood and Lightning*. In his description of the two books as, respectively, "a novel of expectation," and "a novel of exasperation,"[13] Aldecoa suggested a common narrative foundation of *tempo lento* and suspense. Sebastián Vázquez knows from the outset that he is doomed, and simply postpones the moment of capitulation. The time of the action is unreal and figurative: "Monday: death, Tuesday: fear, Wednesday: calm, Thursday: sadness, Friday: blood ties" (252), and cannot provide for any improvement in his situation. An imposing sense of aimlessness and inevitability cancels out any impression of dynamism fostered by Sebastián's social encounters and his flight through time and space.

Two critics have found fault in the construction of *With the East Wind*. One objects to the reader's knowing virtually from the outset how the book will end.[14] It may be argued in reply to this criticism that the reader's foreknowledge is in fact an advantage, since it forces him to accept the inevitable motivation of the plot, and thereby converts him into an accomplice of fate. Another complains that the novel is imbalanced and contains some passages of padding which, among other things, impair its effectiveness as an exercise in suspense.[15] However, in the overall context of the work, certain scenes, characters, and events which may at first appear superfluous are in reality part of a system of dramatic contrast. For example, the prolonged scene in which Sebastián reluctantly witnesses a conversation between Cabeda and the confirmed political activist, Hernández, throws into relief his disorientation and passivity. The various characters with whom he comes into contact are less a stream of fleeting acquaintances than a series of alternative philosophies and options of behavior. Finally, a large proportion of the last chapter depicting the annual festivities of a Castilian country village is more than a neo-costumbrist tableau providing comic relief: the setting thus described is one of traditional routine and cultural normality from which Sebastián is tellingly excluded.

Any residual impression of untidiness or faulty construction in *With the East Wind* may be dispelled by consulting Sobejano's defense of the novel's artistic unity.[16]

As in *Blood and Lightning,* Aldecoa makes much use here of foreshadowing, irony, and imagery. The first section of the narrative, just over three pages in length, closes with a warning from La Carola, the brothel owner, to her boisterous clients: "I lock up at three o'clock: now you know. I don't want any trouble with the police" (10). Next morning, Sebastián finds an unlucky horseshoe as he and Larios enter the site where the fair is to be held, and a peasant foretells their clash with the police. There is somber irony in Pepita's throw-away remark about "the four days or so of one's life" (111) at a time when Sebastián has only four days of freedom left, and in Argensola's explanation that, had it not been for Sebastián's company, he would never have given Roque a lift to Cogolludo, because he looked like a potential murderer.

The most prominent of the many images which enrich the text is the folkloric motif of the east wind. Carlisle has noted how the motif acquires increasingly unpleasant connotations with death and decay, and becomes "the metaphorical agent of alienation."[17] A less frequent, but equally powerful series of images evokes the cruel struggle for survival in the world of nature. A hawk circles over a flock of frightened rabbits as Sebastián sleeps uneasily in the open countryside; a spider waits patiently for a fly to fall into its web. In the penultimate chapter the images of a scorpion devoured by its mate and an owl lost without its female companion point up Sebastián's loneliness and sexual despair. Other images which substantiate the novel's themes are those which treat of the value of human life in terms of money. The motifs of gambling with one's life, and of paying for one's mistakes figure in this category.

Further aspects of style include litanylike enumerations and rich conceits. Some passages in *With the East Wind* feature up to nine items, enumerating the properties of the east wind, the behavior of various animals at a particular time of day, or a range of activities in a Madrid bar. In the following sequence, a crucial change of tense and person in the verb of the final unit brings out forcefully the inevitability of Sebastián's capture or surrender:

En cuanto llegara a Madrid tendría, lo sentía en el cuerpo, el miedo de la persecución. Madrid era muy grande pero acabarían cogiéndole. En Madrid encontraría ayuda en los amigos, pero acabarían cogiéndole. En

Madrid uno cree perderse en un nubarro de gente, pero acaban cogiéndote. En Madrid. . . . (76)

He could feel in his bones that as soon as he got to Madrid he would experience the fear of being hunted. Madrid was very big, but they would catch him in the end. In Madrid he would get help from friends, but they would catch him in the end. In Madrid you think you can lose yourself in the crowd, but they always catch you in the end. In Madrid. . . .

Conceits like those used to describe Sebastián and Pepita's spicy conversation when they first meet demonstrate a highly developed creative facility with words:

En los amagos del belén está el salero. En los dichos barrocos, platicando, está enredador y camelante el diablo pequeñajo, perilla chivona, colita de ratón, barriga de tambor, que zurce los pecados de la carne. Sebastián sabe demasiado. Pepita sabe demasiado. Acaban dejando el juego, empatado de golferías, triste de ingenios viejos, plateresco de las imágenes de la germanía.

Although this passage defies translation as a whole, its flavor can be captured by rendering certain isolated phrases into English. The artful couple "score the same number of points in their match of innuendo," and construct "a plateresque frieze made up of the images of popular speech." García Viñó rightly claims that there are few present-day Spanish writers capable of matching Aldecoa's mastery of the metaphor.

The same can be said of his sensitivity to idiom and dialect. In *With the East Wind* he faithfully represents the unique language spoken by the Gypsies. García Viñó has listed many of the terms of *caló* which appear in Sebastián's dialogue with Larios, el Langó, and other Gypsy acquaintances.[18] While these terms certainly reinforce an overall impression of verisimilitude, they function primarily as indices of the peculiarity of Gypsy culture. Sebastián's drunken lapse into *caló* before surrendering to the police signals a desperate last-minute attempt at self-assertion through the nostalgic recall of a vanishing identity. The change in language at this point lends emphasis to the central theme of cultural conflict and alienation.

IV *Critical Appraisal of the First Two Novels*

Blood and Lightning and *With the East Wind* together established Aldecoa as a central figure in the development of the Spanish novel in the 1950s. Melchor Fernández Almagro and Carlos Gortari praised the freshness and vitality with which he portrayed the realities of Spain.[19] His achievement was enhanced in the eyes of another critic because he had avoided the pitfalls of costumbrism and transcended the level of the commonplace.[20] These opinions must have given him particular satisfaction, since his expressed aim in this projected trilogy was to give a verisimilar representation of contemporary provincial Castile by broadening the range of realistic literature. Eugenio de Nora, however, expressed disappointment that *With the East Wind* conveyed a rather superficial impression of Spain.[21]

The emphasis given to local or national factors detracts from the universality of the situations and experiences depicted in the two books. *With the East Wind* is nevertheless ample evidence that Aldecoa possessed a personal view of the human condition. The ideas that life is a gamble, that man is a potential victim of fate, and that solitude, responsibility, and alienation are part and parcel of human existence acquire a certain prominence. They are shortly taken up again and applied on a truly universal scale in *Great Sole*.

Aldecoa's experiment with archetypal symbolism in *With the East Wind* proved successful. The potential of metaphorical design is shown to even greater effect in *Great Sole,* where it is again an appropriate medium for conveying the author's world view. Other technical features to be carried over from the first two novels and developed in the third and fourth include: the description of weather conditions as a sustained metaphor and reinforcement of the plot; the use of foreshadowing to achieve an intriguing sense of fatality; the cultivation of irony as a means of establishing pathos; and interior duplication, which will have a crucial and organic function in determining the meaning of *Great Sole* and *Part of a Story.* Aldecoa's subsequent refinement of such devices takes some of the force out of the criticism that he paid disproportionate attention to matters of technique at the start of his career.

In *Blood and Lightning* and *With the East Wind* the author also attained high standards in style and characterization. His stylistic virtuosity has been illustrated sufficiently above. The studies of María Ruiz and Ernesta Arenas, and of Sebastián Vázquez and José Cabeda, evidence his intelligent and sensitive treatment of character. We can conclude with Eugenio de Nora that "From the very start Aldecoa strikes us as an astonishingly mature novelist."[22]

CHAPTER 5

The Third Novel: Gran Sol

I *Analysis of Plot and Content*

IN his essay "A Sea of Tales,"[1] Aldecoa lamented the absence of a Spanish tradition of literature about the sea. *Gran Sol (Great Sole)* is intended to redress this grievance. Dedicated "to the men who work the fishing run in the area between forty-eight and fifty-six degrees latitude north and six and fourteen degrees longitude west, the waters of Great Sole," the novel is in part the fruit of Aldecoa's experience with the crew of a fishing vessel in that area. His accurate use of marine terminology and close attention to professional and geographical detail create a sound impression of verisimilitude. But as in *Blood and Lightning,* the author's main concern is to study the behavior of a human group in limited surroundings, and to define the psychological and moral significance of a disruption in their routine experience brought about by an accident.

The narrative of *Great Sole* combines studied monotony with drama. Two ships, the *Uro* and the *Aril,* set out from Gijón, a port on the Cantabrian coast of Spain. There are hopes of a good catch in spite of the omnipresent threat of stormy weather. Out at sea the sailors pass the time in routine chores and conversation about banal, day-to-day topics (chapters 2–3). On the third day away from land, this monotony is interrupted when the two ships cast their nets but have to wait until the following afternoon before hauling in their catch, in a tense period of skillful and strenuous activity. A dramatic scene follows in which Simón Orozco, the captain in charge of fishing in the *Aril,* orders two of his crew to tear a muraena, or shark, to pieces with boat hooks. The sixth chapter describes the events of the fifth day spent at sea. In spite of the increasingly stormy weather, Simón orders the crew to cast the net once more, only to see it become entangled in the propeller. With night falling upon them, the two boats make for Bantry on the southern coast of Ireland, eventually reaching the safety of dry land after twenty-four hours of uncomfortable suspense. The first of the novel's two parts is brought to a conclusion by the seventh chapter which tells of the crew's brief, though entertaining, stay at Bantry. A scuffle between Macario Martín, the cook, and Joaquín Sas, his kitchen aid, stands out as the only real event in the chapter, but also serves to highlight Simón Orozco's thoughtful visit to the cemetery where Spanish sailors who have died at sea are buried. The final paragraphs inform us that the *Uro* and the *Aril,* now repaired, have left Ireland for the second leg of their outward journey, heading northward to the fishing grounds.

Monotony is reinstated in the opening chapter of part 2, as various characters have no alternative but to fill the temporal void with daydreams, reminiscences of childhood and wartime experience, considerations about their families, and deliberations on possible retirement. Next day, fog and rain have given way to sunlight and the men return to their communal work repairing the nets. The narrative receives a temporary injection of unpleasantly vivid color when Macario Martín, Joaquín Sas, and Domingo Ventura catch a number of sea birds, skin, and cook them for the crew's midday meal. "Habitual weariness, boredom and emptiness"[2] return, until the *Uro* makes an outstanding catch. The following day it is the *Aril's* turn to draw in the nets, with the same favorable result. After the fish have been cleaned and stored, a second incident occurs in which Simón Orozco vents his sadistic wrath on a muraena (chapter 10).

In the next chapter a severe deterioration in weather conditions does not deter the *patrón* from ordering the fishing to continue, in spite of obvious danger. However, this time he takes one chance too many and pays for his impetuosity with his life: in an attempt to prevent the heavy net falling on top of Macario Martín, Simón is himself caught by it and crushed against the side of the ship. The accident leaves him helpless and mortally injured. The remainder of the eleventh and the greater part of the twelfth chapter prolong Simón Orozco's agony and death, made especially pathetic by the relentless violence of the elements which allow him no peaceful rest. Five days after leaving Bantry and with at least six hours of sailing required to reach the safety of Irish soil again (on page 180 the distance is estimated to be one hundred miles), he dies. In the novel's closing scene, the *Uro* and the *Aril* are mere specks on the horizon as they pursue their homeward journey to Spain, having buried their captain "in a wind-swept corner of the graveyard" (201) at Bantry.

Pace Manuel García Viñó and Otto Fischer, who regard the novel as having an undifferentiated multiple protagonist,[3] it is clear that Simón Orozco enjoys a position of prominence. A human conflict is deftly defined throughout *Great Sole* which especially concerns him. As the *patrón de pesca* he is responsible for ship and crew, but a sense of urgency and impatience characterizes him from the outset. His first reported words, to Carmelo Alvarez, are "How much longer must we wait?" (14). He nearly loses his temper soon after with Domingo Ventura, the engineer, at a nearby tavern. A symbolic passage then describes him as a gambler and one who might take chances: "Simón Orozco was lying on his bunk, calculating whether the coin each wave carried would come out heads or tails; he made calculations with the compass as if it were a roulette wheel, and let his decision depend on the way it might spin" (46). He also has a mania for routine and punctuality but behaves inconsistently; he is prone to bouts of depression, and on two occasions is gripped with an insane hatred for the parasitical muraena. Throughout the story Simón Orozco is, above all, vulnerable. Yet his customary melancholy and recklessness are not the only factors contributing to the accident which kills him. A new psychological element appears, an altruistic impulse to sacrifice himself for Macario Martín at the crucial moment when the overloaded net threatens the cook in its fall. Complaining that the equipment was not strong enough, the injured Simón admits with a measure of stoical humility that "Accidents happen because we make mistakes..." (182). His final words, reluctant and fatalistic, are "The sea is to blame. It had to happen one day" (185), and the last order he gives to his crew, that for safety's sake they should heel to — "hacer capa" — thereby prolonging the journey to the nearest port, illustrates the same spirit of subdued heroism and self-denial: by so delaying the ship's return, he must surely die.

Great Sole, then, may be viewed as a realistic novel which presents a credible human drama in verisimilar circumstances. But it also possesses further dimensions of myth and metaphor, along with a certain parabolic quality through which Aldecoa articulates his conception of morality and human destiny. As Gonzalo Sobejano has observed, "*Great Sole* expresses highly evocative mythical themes."[4] The text bears a preface in the form of a quote from the book of Luke. Orozco is likened unto the biblical figure of Simon Peter whose legendary impetuosity, fallibility, and vocation for martyrdom he simulates. His obsession with the muraena and defiance of the elements are epic features which Manuel García Viñó recognizes in his description of the novel as "an exaltation, in epic style, of an unknown and heroic struggle between man and the environment."[5] The first fishing catch is related in inspired terms which reinforce a mythical interpretation: "The north wind threatens. The north wind gives warning. The roar of the waves is the roar of multitudes. The noise of the waves is the noise of prehistoric cataclysms, of the biblical cataclysm. The waves were already roaring and the north wind buffeting. After four hours Simón Orozco gave the order for the net to be drawn in" (101). Orozco's behavior is thus set in an archetypal mold of universal concern.

Great Sole perpetuates the tradition of stories about the sea which includes works like *Moby Dick, The Ancient Mariner,* and *The Old Man and the Sea.* There are similarities in plot, theme, and conception between Aldecoa's novel and those of Melville and Hemingway. Simón Orozco, Captain Ahab, and Santiago, the modest hero of Hemingway's novella, are all defeated in a contest with nature. Ahab pursues the white whale; Orozco and Santiago have to contend with the omnipresent and sinister threat of sharks. The actions of all three men form part of what Ishmael, the narrator of *Moby Dick,* calls "the grand programme of Providence."[6] In their respective ventures, the men are obliged to come to terms with their destiny, gauging the influence of fate and the extent of their free will. There is a universal dimension to each of their struggles: characters and settings are endowed with symbolic meaning.

A parabolic function is also common to the three books. One of the characters in *Great Sole,* Venancio Artola, actually tells some stories which he calls "parables." His allegorical narratives impart morals which the other crew members find unintelligible. The reader or critic of *Great Sole* is required to make a greater mental effort to interpret the moral implicit in Aldecoa's narrative. Yet it is not difficult to see that Simón Orozco is guilty of certain moral transgressions comparable in kind, if not in degree, with those of Captain Ahab, whose "heaven-insulting purpose," "monomaniac revenge," and "fatal pride"[7] are censured in Melville's novel. Orozco is in fact guilty of hubris. An illuminating contrast may be drawn between him and the protagonist of Hemingway's book. Orozco challenges the sea in a spirit of defiance whereas Santiago respects nature's laws and scheme. Santiago loves, admires, and pities the huge fish he hooks, regarding it as his equal and accepting that either one of them may defeat or kill the other. His unpretentious courage and humble endurance stand in stark contrast to Simón Orozco's instability and reckless presumption. Orozco's death, like Ahab's, is consequently seen as retribution for his moral faults.

If Aldecoa suggests the moral significance of his novel through Artola, he dramatizes a personal conception of human destiny in the relation of Simón Orozco to Macario Martín, alias "Matao" ("Stone Dead"). This nickname is by no means fortuitous, since the ambiguity, irony, and ultimate meaning of the novel stem from it. Macario is renowned for his "repentes matones" ("deadly fits of rage," 55), and Mr. O'Halloran, an agent at Bantry, mistakenly addresses him as "Muerto" instead of "Matao." On a previous occasion when Macario got drunk at Bantry, Simón Orozco "almost killed him" (35), and has threatened to repeat that show of discipline if he causes trouble during the present trip. Macario does in fact get drunk and start a fight but it is Simón, and not he, who dies.

A consideration of the role of fate helps to resolve this paradox. Fate has a decisive influence on the men's lives (its importance is indicated by the continuous mention throughout the text of the word "suerte").[8] A picture emerges in *Great Sole* of life as a conjunction of external chance and human adaptation. In this respect, Macario has the gods on his side. His worldly experience, sense of humor, and sociable nature seem to assure him of success and good fortune. He escapes a well-deserved reprimand for causing trouble in O'Neill's bar, and his luck holds good when Simón saves him from the falling net. Orozco, on the other hand, is a fatalist who courts danger, with the inevitable consequence of death. While a combination of personal shortcomings and unlucky breaks partly determines his misfortune, ultimately it is Macario who decides his fate: Simón pays for Macario's transgressions with his life.

Macario actually possesses an eerie, prophetic insight into the workings of fate, life, and death, an insight which turns out to be mysteriously accurate. He believes that no matter how careful a man may be, "There's always someone else waiting for you; you don't realize it, but you're saving things up for him. He's the one who'll kill you, stone dead" (23). This statement explains the symmetrical logic of retribution behind Simón's death. Such a view of the human condition prompts a final analogy with Melville's novel. In chapter 72 of *Moby Dick* Ishmael describes a precarious situation in which he is obliged to hang from the side of the ship at one end of a rope while, at the other end, his Indian friend Queequeg is suspended at sea level, cutting up a whale's carcass. As both men are mutually dependent for their personal safety, Ishmael comes to appreciate "the even-handed equity" of Providence:

> So strongly and metaphysically did I conceive of my situation then, that while earnestly watching his motions, I seemed distinctly to perceive that my own individuality was now merged in a joint stock company of two; that my free will had received a mortal wound; and that another's mistake or misfortune might plunge innocent me into unmerited disaster and death. . . .
> I saw that this situation of mine was the precise situation of every mortal that breathes.[9]

The opinions expressed by Macario and Artola thus situate *Great Sole* in the established tradition of novels of the sea which debate issues of morality and destiny.

II *Aspects of Technique*

The choice of subject matter in *Great Sole* automatically determines the pace, density, and possibilities of development in the story, which is distinguished by the quality of *non multa sed multum* ("little variety but much depth"). Outstanding events are reduced to a minimum, with the result that instead of involving the reader in a dynamic plot, Aldecoa contrives an intricate internal structure which is dense and, above all, rhythmic. The action depicted covers a period of some fifteen days, the first seven of which are accounted for in the seven chapters of the first part. Rhythm varies according to the length of chapters, the amount of time covered during their course, and the amount of action in each. *Tempo lento* is established in the first chapter, where a delay of no more than two or three hours while the *Aril* waits to set sail is described in seventeen pages of text. By contrast, the third chapter, though of the same physical length as the first, depicts the events of a period of at least twelve hours. This atmosphere of monotony is maintained until the fifth chapter, when it is replaced by a sense of dynamism produced by the occurrence of certain events: the first catch, Simón Orozco's rage with the shark, and the accident in which the net is caught in the propeller. Tension is then relieved in chapter 7 which relates the crew's adventures at Bantry.

The same rhythmic pattern of slow crescendo, leading up to a major event (accident), followed by a prolonged coda, runs through the second part of *Great Sole*. The opening chapter is an unprecedented twenty-four pages in length, of which the first fifteen account for a period of about eight hours from dawn to midday. At the end of the chapter the *Uro* and the *Aril* are still heading northward, the slowness of their progress symbolized by the use of an almost identical phrase to describe their location at the end of both chapters 7 and 8. Simón's accident, the major articulation of the plot, occurs in the fourth of seven chapters in the second part, at a point when seventy-six percent of the narrative of that part and eighty-eight percent of the whole have elapsed. The three remaining chapters prolong and complete the story, growing progressively shorter as if to give formal expression to the experience of agony and death. The rhythm of the novel is allowed to continue uninterrupted in an open-ended fashion. The development of *Great Sole* is a paradigm of sensitive control and fine balance throughout.

This structural coherence is enhanced by the constant attention to weather conditions, so that the human drama is set in a dynamic natural context. Nature's rhythm is a symphonic accompaniment to the sailor's activity and experience. A storm's building up and breaking is a metaphor and analogue of the plot, as in *Blood and Lightning*. It is imminent in the first chapter of *Great Sole;* when the ships eventually leave the harbor, the first drops of rain start to fall from a black sky. Out at sea, the weather is generally bad and deteriorates as the plot progresses, until in chapter 6 the north wind is blowing like a hurricane. It is at this juncture that the first accident occurs, at the heart of Great Sole and with the storm at its peak. Similarly in the second part, weather conditions are critical when Simón is crushed by the net. Aldecoa then chooses not to relax the level of suspense, and instead depicts the growing violence of wind and rain in order to emphasize the gravity of Simón's situation. When the captain eventually dies, "the north wind suddenly blew even more strongly and the rain was like an impenetrable deafening wall" (193). Reference to the weather is used as a deliberate means of creating and prolonging tension throughout the novel.

The two parts of *Great Sole* stand in a relation of flexible symmetry. Each contains seven chapters with a similar distribution of events: fishing catch, attack on a shark, storm, and accident. Simón visits Bantry cemetery in chapter 7 and is buried there at the close of the novel when the ship makes a second call, after a similar period at sea. An item like the BBC radio news appears once in each part. This structural repetition produces various effects. It creates a balanced artistic pattern or shape; it renders the monotony of life on board a deep sea fishing vessel; and, as Jack Jelinski has noted, it suggests the cyclical nature of existence itself.[10]

Patterning is also achieved by the consistent use of certain motifs, and by narrative foreshadowing. The text is punctuated by a number of passages dealing with sea birds such as the petrel and albatross and their significance in sailors' lore. The themes of good luck and the idea of a shipwreck are recurrent features in conversation. For example, the adjective "náufrago", meaning "shipwrecked," appears in only the second paragraph of the work, and the noun "naufragio" figures in the narrative of chapter 3, in a dialogue between Sas, Artola, and Ugalde in chapter 7, and again in the narrative of chapter 8. At the level of formal expression, an identical binary construction is used throughout to introduce the two Quiroga brothers: "the clean-shaven one, the other with a gray beard" (95); "the one with the big hands, and the one with finger nails like black beetles" (112).

Foreshadowing is once more a procedure basic to Aldecoa's technique. In addition to their structural, unifying function, omens and predictions relate to the theme of fate and frequently serve as a vehicle for the expression of irony. The narrative of *Great Sole* includes "auguries" and numerous "bad signs" (86) which are generally related to the weather conditions and may be interpreted by a superstitious sailor like Carmelo Alvarez. Carmelo's intuition at the beginning of the voyage, that "This is going to be a good trip; something inside tells me so" (15), is proved nonetheless relevant for its tragic inaccuracy. Other characters offer words of advice which appear especially significant in retrospect, especially Koldobika's warning about the dangerous conditions along latitude fifty-six in the Great Sole area. It is poignantly ironic that Simón Orozco should skeptically dismiss such warnings as "prophetic magic" (15). Some predictions surprise the reader by their detail and exactness. In chapter 5 Macario anticipates the first accident when he tells the crew in the poop "If you get the net caught up in the propeller today [Simon] will really give you a row, and rightly so" (76). Others are remarkable for their unwittingly prophetic nature, especially as regards Simón's fate. Joaquín Sas viciously remarks that "You can't sail with him without some upset or other.... I hope he's killed, and Afá along with him" (71). The fulfillment of predictions, or narrative foreshadowing, is an important poetic feature of *Great Sole*.

Aldecoa's narrative technique, or method of presenting reality, is more complex than many critics have supposed. Gonzalo Torrente Ballester expressed the surprising opinion, repeated by Ricardo Senabre and others, that *"Great Sole* is more akin to reportage than to the novel."[11] Aldecoa's firsthand experience of the conditions aboard a deep-sea fishing vessel, his exact observation of highly specialized activities, and his respect for precise details of cartography and geography would go some way toward substantiating this view. Such facts might also be invoked to describe *Great Sole* as a neo-costumbrist novel, in the vein of Camilo José Cela's travelogues. Eugenio de Nora discerns "a possible critical or social intention,"[12] while Manuel García Viñó suggests that Aldecoa "is critically reviewing the fishermen's social position," and "is certainly denouncing [their lot]."[13] However, García Viñó immediately qualifies his assertion by adding that such a view of the novel is quite insufficient, since in the craft of fiction creative imagination and poetic technique complement and transcend any testimonial objective. Aldecoa's indignation at the fact that "A malicious review categorized *Great Sole* as a documentary"[14] is a clear indication of his adherence to this literary principle.

In *Great Sole* Aldecoa employs a varied and sophisticated method involving pseudoobjective presentation, direct authorial statement, indirect interior monologue, humor and irony, poetic stylization, and a subtle cult of obscurity. A quality of cinematic objectivity may be found in some passages where the author attempts to account for perceptible detail. But the narrator invariably breaks the illusion of objectivity with an adverbial or adjectival phrase which betrays identification and interpretation on his part. The following passage of static description is an illustration. "Begoña Maria's hair was brown, a light and lusterless shade of brown. The skin in the corner of her eyelids was wrinkled. Two deep furrows ran across her cheeks, starting from her mouth which was pursed in bitterness" (25).

The text contains some passages of direct, and apparently omniscient, commentary, like those referring to the presence of a *patraña,* or false lead, in every journey, or to the communal task of repairing the nets (77–78, and 150–51). Interior monologue is used occasionally as a substitute for explicit psychological description, for example, in an analysis of Juan Ugalde's thoughts included in chapter 3:

> Juan Ugalde stroked the belaying pins of the steering wheel with the inside of his hand. . . . He thought his captain Simón Orozco had been mistaken. He had sailed on American ships since he was a boy. He didn't have an exact idea, but knew it had been for a long time. Things went well for him on the American ships, so why did he leave them? His captain Simón Orozco had been mistaken. He wouldn't have left. (50–51)

The deliberate confusion of third-person subject forms creates an apposite air of uncertainty about Simón Orozco.

The predominantly grave tenor of the narrative is offset by moments of humor. In spite of his sinister role in the dramatic plot, Macario Martín often adds a note of comedy to the action, as when he imitates a dog for the company's amusement at Mr. O'Halloran's. A more grotesque instance of Macario's behavior is additionally humorous because of the way in which it is presented: "Simón Orozco has found a place to sit on top of a crate . . . which was once used as a cage for a ringed dove, until Macario Martín ate it for his tea" (54). Examples of strictly verbal humor are also found in *Great Sole,* and generally involve the comic repetition of a word or phrase.

Irony pervades the work, as we have already noted. Simón's words and actions rebound on him constantly, as on the occasion when he tells Castro, "The truth is, I want to leave the sea as much as anyone, because I've had enough and would like to stay at home with my wife and children. . . . I'm always saying this'll be my last year, that I'm going to quit the sea. . ." (141). The unfortunate phrase "You can make a living out of fishing" (188), pronounced by Celso Quiroga while Simón is dying, is another illustration of the novel's persistent ambiguity.

Some sections of *Great Sole* possess a poetic quality deriving from the use of imagery along with certain rhetorical figures and syntactic constructions. Ornate in some places, laconic and rigorous in other, the language everywhere bears the mark of elegance and artifice. The specialized vocabulary of the sea is both verisimilar and evocative, and the narrator constantly uses that idiom metaphorically: "Joaquín Sas extendió la red de la murmuración"

("Joaquín Sas extended the net of gossip," 79); "A veces le entraba una idea golfa de tirarlo todo a barlovento en vino y en mujeres" ("He sometimes had the wild idea of throwing all his money overboard on wine and women," 176). *Iteratio,* asyndeton, and two, three, four, even six part structures abound, creating effects of symmetry and contrast which enrich the sense conveyed: "Olía a podredumbre de algas y a tormenta" ("There was a smell of rotten seaweed and storm," 13); "La mar a los costados del barco era una gigante, musculosa oscuridad, que amenazaba, acariciaba o golpeaba el casco" ("The sea all around was a black, muscular giant threatening, caressing or battering the vessel like a shell," 33).

These properties of artifice and stylization are accentuated by an overall procedure of insinuation and a cult of ambiguity or mystery. *Great Sole* is a novel of subtle clues, deft hints, and underlying secrets, which needs to be approached with the same careful attention as *El Jarama* by Rafael Sánchez Ferlosio. When interviewed by Julio Trenas in 1957, Aldecoa placed surprisingly little emphasis on "certain obscure symbolism" in his novel.[15] He nevertheless instructs the reader how to interpret *Great Sole* by including in the text some reflexive allusions to the acts of telling stories and reading novels.

Juan Arenas is upset to think some people might consider him "an unconvincing storyteller." "[He] was telling a tale about the war and pretending he'd been a coward, but he always managed to figure prominently at the right moments, when the danger was greatest" (59). Simón Orozco enjoys identical, if contrived, prominence in the novel: he is the first and last character to be mentioned, he often appears in an unobtrusively highlighted position, "standing silently on his own" (21), and he is the object of most ironical comments. Aldecoa's credibility as a narrator and Simón's reckless courage are confirmed in this instance of interior duplication. A similar analogy between an apparently random tale and the primary narrative is to be found in Macario Martín's "story about a storm off Estaca de Vares." He assures the company that, although the story may appear farfetched, it is based on an actual event. José Afá regards it as "the finest tale I've heard about the sea in all my life" (38), possibly a vicarious piece of boasting on Aldecoa's behalf. Venancio Artola, in whose name it is tempting to find a partial anagram or echo of the author's, has a particular style "which makes the most improbable elements [of a story] seem ambiguous and difficult to understand, almost ridiculous, almost profound and comic'' (88); it is an accurate reflection of Aldecoa's complex narrative technique.

The author indirectly rejects a facile and mimetic, and especially a costumbrist, reading of the novel when he gently satirizes "the summer tourist on the lookout for something picturesque" who spends his time eating and drinking in silence on the quayside (17). Other attitudes are equally unacceptable: Domingo Ventura has an untutored and wayward imagination, Gato Rojo finds novels a bore, and Joaquín Sas is unable to penetrate beyond the literal surface of a story. The ideal approach is advocated by Venancio Artola, the specialist in parables. He warns his audience that, in order to appreciate his stories fully, they must be willing to "fish for the meaning" (89).

Great Sole is rich in obscurity. In addition to the mystery inherent in the parable of Simón and Macario, the hints that both these men may have been involved in some "secret activity during the war" (64), and the abundance of apparently innocuous, ironical phrases, there are several details which the inadvertent reader might overlook. Certain motifs or phrases recur in an eloquent relation. During a discussion with Macario about the chance which a man who fell overboard would have of surviving, Afá claims that if he were to stay *calm,* the sailor would eventually be rescued. But a cognate form of the word, "calmness" ("serenidad") had been used on the same page to describe Simón Orozco, who "has a calm, serene air" (126). Simón is compared with the hypothetical individual who is the victim of an accident, such ambiguity deriving from an arrangement of syntax. Some motifs are inherently equivocal. Sharks are a sinister symbol for the parasitical relation between two human beings. When one is wounded, its fellows are attracted by "the blood of a brother" (91); thus Simón dies for Macario, who sees man preying on his fellowman. A formal device like the open ending of chapter 13, displayed by the inconclusive points, silently draws attention to Macario Martín's cryptic role in the novel: "Gato Rojo opened out his hands, opened the air around him as if it were a book. — Macario. . ." (200).

III   *Conclusion*

On the basis of his success in *Great Sole,* Jack Jelinski asserts that "Aldecoa cannot be considered as just another novelist of the fifties; he is a master-craftsman of the genre who has elaborated a fictional world uniquely his own.''[16] *Great Sole* certainly articulates a personal vision of human existence on a universal plane. Aldecoa's experience on board a Spanish fishing vessel inspired an imaginative inquiry into transcendental questions of morality and destiny, which could best be conducted in the symbolic medium of the sea novel. The wealth of association and suggestion in *Great Sole* is a measure of the depth of that inquiry, and an indication of the technical maturity which Aldecoa has now attained.

CHAPTER 6

The Fourth Novel: Parte de una historia

I *Introductory Remarks*

Parte de una historia (*Part of a Story*) is Aldecoa's last novel and the result of many years of careful preparation. A polyfaceted work, it has confused a number of critics who, in myopic insistence on isolated features, have often underestimated its complex unity, and in more than one instance, even misunderstood its very status as a work of fiction. There are really several ways of categorizing *Part of a Story*; each of these perspectives is legitimate and all are mutually complementary.

First, the novel originates in Aldecoa's experience of life on a small island in the Canaries archipelago. The reappearance of the narrator in an island community after an absence of four years, corresponds to Aldecoa's own return to La Graciosa in the spring of 1961, following his first visit at the beginning of 1957. Second, *Part of a Story* is a document of social realism which provides a verisimilar account of life and customs on one of the Spanish islands. One critic has succinctly defined the work as an example of "updated *costumbrismo*."[1] At the same time, Aldecoa contrasts the values of urban, technological society with those of primitive civilization and treats of the theme of the pastoral illusion. Third, the book is a psychological study of alienation and an investigation of the narrator's emotional and moral traumas. The ideas of solidarity, isolation, and guilt are central in this respect. Finally, in this novel Aldecoa puts across his tragic view of the human condition, recapitulating the themes of responsibility, retribution, and destiny expressed in previous works.

A multidimensional narrative technique is employed to convey these many levels of meaning. The characters, plot, and setting are endowed with symbolic significance, and many images and motifs are ambivalent. The first-person form of presentation is an ambiguous medium exploited to great effect. Interior duplication, involving a critique of style and rhetoric, illuminates the book's status as a work of fiction.

II   *Analysis of Action and Content*

The action of *Part of a Story* is set on a small island in the Atlantic ocean and is narrated by an enigmatic individual whose only sign of identity is the anonymous first-person subject pronoun form. More of a spectator than a protagonist, he relates a series of incidents which occur during his stay with the islanders. In chapter 5 their peaceful life, with which the narrator has become integrated, is interrupted by the washing up on their shores of a wrecked vessel carrying four drunken Americans. These "náufragos" immediately associate with two English people already resident on the island, and over the next ten chapters the outsiders, collectively referred to as "los chonis," proceed to disrupt the community life with their excessive drinking, wild spending, and relaxed sexual mores. Chapters 16 to 20 describe the death by drowning and eventual burial of Jerry, who rashly goes swimming when drunk on the night of a carnival. The *chonis* subsequently quit the island, leaving the inhabitants to return to their customarily hard-working existence. Two chapters later the narrator brings the book to a close, announcing his own impending departure.

Gregorio Salvador has suggested the extent to which *Part of a Story* may be considered an autobiographical documentary.[2] The use of the first-person narrative method freely invites this interpretation. Although he foregoes an analysis of the relation between author and narrator — an exercise which might have yielded some interesting insights into Aldecoa's personality — Salvador identifies a plethora of elements in the novel as corresponding to specific realities which the author would have encountered during his visit to the island. The names and identity of people, places, and even of boats tie *Part of a Story* inescapably to La Graciosa. Of particular interest is Salvador's revelation that an American yacht actually ran aground on La Graciosa when Aldecoa was there. This critic's investigations in the field lead him to the conclusion that *Part of a Story* is a descriptive chronicle devoid of invention. Reductive and oversimplified though it may be, Salvador's view is an indispensable point of reference.

If the characters and their setting are regarded in a general light, then the novel takes on the appearance of a verisimilar recreation of the social habits and characteristics of an island community such as that of La Graciosa. Aldecoa's deliberate practice of not specifying the island by name is perhaps evidence that he wished the novel to be read as something more than an autobiographical documentary limited by considerations of time and space. The reality he describes is typical of an area and social order. He presents a tableau, alternately romantic and down to earth, of life in a fishing community where, in "the daily maritime adventure,"[3] the sailors risk their lives in a contest with nature. As the narrator observes, "This is an island of work" (36). The small community is organized in a loose hierarchy, with Roque, who owns a boat and runs a store, a benevolent patriarchal figure. It is founded on fixed conventions of morality and lore. The issue of sexual behavior is highlighted in a subplot which follows the romance between the promiscuous Beatrice and Domingo, a young islander who is engaged to a local girl. This brief affair is a serious challenge to accepted marital customs, compromising reputations and family ties. Other events indicate the role of tradition and lore in this society. The arrival of a catch of fish at the harbor, for example, is accompanied by a ritual ceremony. When Maestro Juan lands a great catch of herring, the community joins in the task of cleaning the fish, and show their contentment "in a barely audible chorus, intoning a song whose words cannot be made out" (69). The epithets "primitive," "milleniary," and "elementary" describe such subliminal manifestations of communal behavior.

The dominant social theme treated in this novel is that of the opposition between modern urban and primitive values. The characters represent different cultures. An array of objects found in the cabin of the Americans' luxury yacht includes record sleeves, glossy magazines, packets of cigarettes, and bottles of liquor, and symbolizes the acquisitive consumer society from which they come. From the islanders' point of view, the *chonis'* values are, quite simply, decadent. Even the food they eat at breakfast time is taken as a sign of frivolity and ostentation. They are apparently indifferent to the sexual infidelity of a partner, and are generally irresponsible. With justification, an American critic has complained that the image here projected of his compatriots is one-sided and superficial.[4]

For the sake of clarity in his argument and for dramatic effect,

Aldecoa resorted to a method of antithesis in order to illustrate the relative merits and demerits of urban and primitive civilizations. His vision of the local community is accordingly biased. Although he does not shrink from portraying the pettiness and interfering ways of some of the islanders, the overall picture he paints of them is rose-colored. Their rude life-style and unassuming work ethic command his admiration. Their unfailing solidarity with their own kind, and their civilized generosity to the *chonis* after Jerry has drowned are seen as exemplary virtues. An eloquent example of the contrast between the two groups may be found in the portrayal of two female characters, Beatrice and Enedina, Roque's wife. Beatrice's ambiguous morality and dedication to the trivial pursuits of the *dolce vita* are overshadowed by Enedina's spirit of self-sacrifice as housewife and mother. In spite of the obvious naivety of his vision, Aldecoa's account of human values on the island is highly evocative.

The narrator stands midway between the two groups. He is a city man who, on his first night on the island, is disconcerted by the early hour at which the islanders retire to bed. In a dramatic monologue in chapter 7 he remembers the life of confusion and unrest he has left behind. But as early as the morning after his arrival, he identifies with the local people, referring unpretentiously to "our island." His willingness to accept the inconveniences of life in a primitive setting, and his capacity for responding to the beauties of the landscape augur well for him. The sight of daybreak, in chapter 13, fills his soul with tranquillity. Yet he cannot help identifying also with the *chonis*. The English couple, David and Laurel, attract his attention first, but it is Jerry, the leader of the American party, who interests him most because in Jerry he recognizes a kindred spirit.

At root, the narrator is a refugee from urban civilization and a victim of alienation, both social and existential. He is susceptible to the pastoral illusion, because he suffers from a malaise originating in his urban past. There are two degrees to his social alienation. At a local level, he is conscious of a sophistication which makes him incompatible with the islanders. He feels uncomfortably conspicuous, like an interfering foreigner, on a trip to a lighthouse with Roque and two other men. In a broader context, he is estranged from society at large and looks on his temporary stay on the island as an escape from a threatening urban environment on the Spanish mainland. Other instances of the "escape" motif suggest that the narrator's alienation is also existential. On the fourth night of his stay on the island he walks alone to the beach and, sitting down next to a boat, reflects on his situation:

I am on the island once more and on the run. Who am I running away from? I could not say. Everything is too confused.... And am I here because there is something for me to find here? I could not say. The escape itself is maybe enough to explain being on the run. And I am here next to this boat, alone in the night. And, like this boat, am I bound for no fixed destination for ever? (35)

These feelings of existential unrest oppress him during the whole of his stay on the island. He feels helpless in his isolation, a condition which Roque rightly diagnoses as an illness of the soul. Even expressions of solidarity from the most well-disposed of the islanders are no cure for his spiritual suffering.

The cause of this trouble is a mysterious moral dilemma. The narrator gives the impression of being haunted by a shameful secret which he cannot bring himself to confess. Chapter 8 closes with a prolonged meditation on the theme of moral justification, salvation, and damnation. Then in chapter 11 he tries to evade the embarrassing issue of his drunkenness of the night before. But his memory will not allow his conscience to rest, and threatens to revive what he provocatively calls a "retrospective guilt" (103). This sense of moral trauma is one of the book's most compelling qualities.

The narrator is drawn toward the *chonis* because he discovers in them a reflection of his own existential unrest and moral confusion. Their accident and reckless conduct strike him as an alluring paradigm of human behavior. He sees the shipwreck of the *Bloody Mary,* the *chonis'* disruptive stay on the island, and Jerry's death by drowning as parts of a transcendental design for which the only adequate name is "fate." The banal story line thus comes to function as a vehicle for articulating a general conception of man's existence. Human destiny is shown to depend on "the law of the labyrinth" (183). Jerry's experience of being saved from a shipwreck by chance, only to drown some two weeks later, is a singular example of the enigmatic workings of fate.

But the question of responsibility must not be discounted, as is evidenced in a crucial section of chapter 8. For Jerry is the owner and captain of the yacht and, like Simón Orozco in *Great Sole,* the person ultimately responsible for its safe administration. The *Bloody Mary* runs aground because all the people on board are drunk. However, the uniqueness of Jerry's position makes him particularly susceptible to criticism. When he eventually drowns, again as a result of reckless drinking, it is as if he has tempted fate once too often and is being made to pay the price for his repeated transgressions. One of the islanders, Mateo, says as much at the end of chapter 20: "Death has been the price" (209). Notwithstanding the neat symmetry of this scheme of retribution, the narrator argues that there are other, imponderable factors in human destiny. People may be forced by circumstances to assume roles and responsibilities "which do not entirely belong to them" (77). The relation between fate and duty is thus rendered fluid and arbitrary. Man remains in an ambiguous position, charged with shaping his own destiny but permitted to do so only within certain ordained limits.

Part of a Story, like *Great Sole,* is in part a moral fable concerned with ultimate questions such as fate, salvation, and man's responsibility. As such it belongs to a tradition of works such as *Robinson Crusoe, Treasure Island,* and *Naufragios* (*Shipwrecks*) by Alvar Núñez Cabeza de Vaca. Aldecoa's fascination with the myth of Robinson Crusoe is attested by the commentaries he devoted to the theme. His essay "A Sea of Stories" contains a study of "The Five Robinsons" of Defoe, Verne, Salgari, Wyss, and Stevenson, and treats of the exemplary aspect of such works. The weight of this tradition on *Part of a Story* is indicated by the narrator's reference to "the Robinson children of the village" (24), and their education. The Americans and the narrator are in the classic situation of those literary protagonists for whom being stranded on a desert island is a test or education in self-reliance and adaptation to an alien setting.

III   *Aspects of Technique*

The diverse levels of meaning in *Part of a Story* are expressed by a varied narrative technique part mimetic, part symbolic, and part reflexive. A cinematic quality of presentation enhances the effect of a realist or costumbrist work. The narrator actually refers to himself on one occasion as "walking along inside a cinematic documentary" (137). He describes many settings and scenes in plastic terms, as if they were images in an overall picture or design. A consequence of this crudely mimetic approach is the illusion of objectivity in some parts of the text, for example, the endings of chapters 10 and 15, which illustrate the much discussed method of *l'école du regard*. The narrator concludes chapter 10 with the following sentences:

> Domingo y Pedro comienzan una *folía*. . . .
> Yo escucho y bebo ron. Beatrice contempla las manos que rasguean el timple. Gary se apoya en el mostrador junto a Laurel. Maestro Pancho hace humear su cachimba. (100)

> Domingo and Pedro begin to perform a folia. . . .
> I listen and drink rum. Beatrice observes the movement of hands plucking the treble guitar. Gary leans on the counter next to Laurel. Maestro Pancho puffs out smoke from his pipe.

This level of language and presentation is, however, transcended by various elements of the narrative which have a symbolic function. First, the characters: at certain moments the Americans, Jerry, Boby, Beatrice, and Gary, are seen as archetypal. The narrator calls Jerry "a destitute Ulysses on Las Conchas beach" and evokes Dante's allegorical world in his description of Beatrice as "the fallen woman" (71). The characters' experience thus conforms to ancient prototypes like the quest and trial. Both *chonis* and islanders have set roles to play in what is repeatedly termed a "spectacle" or a "performance." In the *chonis'* case this metaphor implies a denunciation of their life-style as an artificial and extravagant farce, but at another level it applies to all involved in the story. Collectively, the islanders fulfill the function of a chorus in this twentieth-century "tragedy" (a word actually employed on page 186). Finally, the characters have roles assigned to them by fate. In the deterministic scheme outlined in the novel, the most prominent figure, Jerry, is expected "to act out his role to the end" (75), as a condition of his destiny.

Second, the plot: the storm which wrecks the *Bloody Mary* and leaves the Americans stranded is a metaphor for the adverse power of fate. To be shipwrecked is therefore to lose one's direction in life. Mateo says that all rich people are shipwrecked, presumably because he considers them corrupt and misguided by materialism. It is significant that at carnival time Jerry should imitate the style of a "pirate" (156), since this identifies him as one who courts danger and challenges authority, in the present instance, the laws of fate.

In this symbolic context the island becomes a haven of security, "a promise of salvation" (74) for those caught on the troubled seas of life. Boats, too, are objects of more than literal significance. A contrast is drawn between Roque's boat, the *Chipirrín,* and the *Bloody Mary,* which not only reflects the difference between the islanders and the *chonis* but also opposes existential security and vitality to alienation and death. The *Chipirrín* is a reliable instrument of work, a humble little craft which has braved many storms and is still seaworthy. The *Bloody Mary* is an expensive plaything which has been destroyed in an absurd accident: now no more than an empty shell, it is personified as a corpse.

The narrator perceives clearly the figurative value of all these objects and situations, since he is himself a sailor on life's troubled waters. In chapter 4 he mentions his "own shipwrecked existence" (41), and later explains his sympathy for Jerry:

He has been shipwrecked — that is the crowning moment of his life for me — .... Even though he may have ridden all the storms in the world — from which I do not exclude the great storm of war, to speak metaphorically — the one that concerns me is the present one, which I have experienced here on the island and he out there, exposed to danger....

Just as the storm has brought Jerry to the island, so the narrator says that the cause of his visit is "another storm, also in the way of a metaphor" (72). He had made equally significant observations in a previous passage:

Looking down from the sand dune, I distinguish two worlds: one behind me, that of the village, and another in front, that of the yacht. These two situations are not only images of what is organized, secure and full of life, and what is disorganized, anarchic and moribund, but diametrically opposed symbols between which I find myself torn. (64–65)

The narrator also identifies with a symbol of security when he compares himself with the *Chipirrín,* thereby expressing the hope that, like the little boat, he will have the strength to face the uncertainties of the future. This symbolic system, built on the motifs of storm, sea, island, and boats, illustrates the central theme of existential alienation with forceful consistency.

Part of a Story is symbolic in a further sense which we have already acknowledged in preceding sections: Aldecoa's narrative about a group of disruptive Americans on an island is also a story about the narrator. In fact, their experience is a correlative of his own. What he refers to as "the objective data" (76) of the narrative — namely, the characters, setting, and events — are images, at one remove, of his situation. Hence our impression of a shadowy, ghostlike figure whose life is intimated to us via a "meta-story." Yet even an analysis of the available "data" does not explain the mystery surrounding the narrator. It is clear that he has been the casualty of a metaphorical storm, and that his stay on the island is therapy for a malaise, but no more information is forthcoming. What he says about other people serves only to confirm our initial illusory impression of him. For example, the qualities of remoteness and "mysterious ambiguity" (106) which he discerns in Laurel and Boby, respectively, describe him with tantalizing exactness. He completely resembles Jerry in that he wears a metaphorical disguise and projects "a distorted image of himself" (141). Yet Jerry, too, is an enigmatic person. There is no way of answering Roque's rhetorical question, "What sort of man can a guy like Jerry be?" (208). Similarly, there is little possibility of discovering who the narrator is, or of identifying the cause of his unrest. The novel seems ultimately to be an illustration of the claim, made by a minor character, that "No one can tell what another person is really like" (104). García Viñó contends that it was Aldecoa's purpose "to induce [in the reader] a sense of existential mystery."[5] This is certainly a positive achievement in the book. Aldecoa's subtle exploitation of the ambiguities inherent in the first-person mode of presentation enabled him to create an atmosphere of uncertainty quite comparable with the oppressive and bewildering mood of Kafka's novels.

The view that *Part of a Story* is primarily a novel about the narrator is further substantiated by the fact that it was provisionally entitled "El vacío" ("The Void") and "El desconocido" ("The Stranger"). "Part of a Story" is nevertheless just as intriguing and eloquent a title. At one level, it reflects the incompleteness of the "data" concerning the Americans, and Jerry in particular: that story is incomplete because it suppresses any reference to the characters' past and future, and confines itself to an account of events which occur in a temporal "parenthesis of inactivity" (76). At another, more fundamental level, the title signals both the nature of the narrator's position in the novel's structure — his story being a loosely outlined part of the whole fiction — and the contrived inconclusiveness of the information regarding him. His story is vague in this way because his life is confused and empty. As Aldecoa himself explained, "I intended to leave the novel open at both ends so that it might show just how much an individual can tell about his own life."[6] The relation of language and life here is in no way accidental. The virtual equivalence between narrative and experience is attested in the word "historia" which in Spanish means both "story" and "history." So, the narrator's account of what happens on the island is no less than a literal "biography," for he is committing his own story and Jerry's "historia vivida" (183) to words.

The complexity of *Part of a Story* is enhanced by Aldecoa's constant practice of interior duplication. Our appreciation of the text as a work of fiction is furthered by those instances in which certain characters in the novel either tell stories or read books. Some stories are told which in various degrees prefigure or mirror the plot of *Part of a Story*. On only the second page of the novel one of the islanders, Casimiro, "tried to tell an amusing tale and spoke of someone who came to search for pirates' treasure on Las Conchas beach and only succeeded in getting drunk" (8). There is somber irony in his remark, for both the narrator and Jerry get drunk at a later stage and fail to discover any treasure, literal or symbolic, in their respective quests. On another occasion Mateo spins a yarn about "valiant innkeepers and epic Don Juans" (137). He challenges Gary to a test of strength in chapter 10; Gary is indeed successful and popular with women, temporarily winning the favors of Laurel.

Part of a Story also contains many observations on style and technique in storytelling. When characters like Mateo and Felix tell stories, they either "exaggerate," "distort," or "adorn" the facts. Only Roque has any respect for objectivity, refusing to melodramatize when, in chapter 4, a storm is imminent and some of the boats are out at sea. Later, he explains the circumstances of the Americans' shipwreck "with the serenity, the mysterious and objective serenity of truth. . ." (61). This nice description of Roque's rhetorical manner underlines in a crucial way the distinction between fact and truth. What ultimately matters in a story is not its factuality — for all stories are "invented to a greater or lesser degree" (137) — but its verisimilitude, a quality which allows mystery and objectivity to exist side by side.

The narrative of *Part of a Story* is itself subjected to direct reflexive analysis. The narrator wonders whether the story of a shipwreck will be credible to those who have not witnessed the event firsthand: "A shipwreck which has nothing to do with the sailors' work is so romantic and unlikely that nobody will believe it. And it is impossible for a drunken crew who survive the wreck to take part in a verisimilar occurrence" (105). He is evidently anxious that his story be accepted as authentic, a concern made especially ironical by Salvador Cajas' elucidations about the novel's basis in fact. At the same time the narrator insists on the story's inherent mystery. In chapter 18 he compares Jerry's story to an abstract and "enigmatic" pattern in a carpet. In his final assessment of the narrative of *Part of a Story,* he asserts its dual nature: "It's the end of this story. A story with an unhappy ending which when told will be lost in time, as if torn from memory, or will have the tangibility and definite outlines of the present or the night before, glowing with the sinister light from the shipwreck and the death which took place during the carnival" (202).

It is a combination of "tangibility" or "objectivity" and "nostalgia" or "mystery" which generates the narrator's "meta-story." He articulates a suppressed confession via the same "strange strategy of self-defense" to which Pepita resorts in the second chapter of *With the East Wind* (113). At an early stage in *Part of a Story* he advises that "Words must be used to conceal" (11), and keeps his personal secret by following that prescription. The bewilderment which such a rhetorical procedure produces in the reader is itself sanctioned in the text, where the act of reading is defined as "something enigmatic." The narrator comments on "the disconcerting hour when, if I take up a book, I get lost in each page, as if reading were something enigmatic. . ." (163).

These reflexive observations and duplicated stories serve two fundamental purposes in *Part of a Story.* They enrich the novel with a poetic context of echoes and reflections in which distinctions between fact and fiction, or between various removes of fiction, are confused, and they encourage the reader's positive response to the inquiry which is conducted in the novel into transcendental issues such as fate and other "mysteries of life" (84). They also guarantee the complex unity of a work in which content and technique are perfectly fused.

The objections that *Part of a Story* evidences "a scarcity of invention,"[7] and that it is not fiction but a documentary,[8] can therefore be dismissed, along with the assertion that the plot should not have been extended beyond the limits of a short story.[9] *Part of a Story* is a novel both in form and in kind. A further criticism, that

"The plot of the book is hardly relevant or even important"[10] also requires qualification. Artificiality or superficiality of plot is not in itself a reason for disparagement. In *Part of a Story* a plot based on clichés functions as a framework within which symbolic structures are elaborated and transcendental themes discussed. Only a limited and typecast view of the genre can give cause for regret such as that expressed here: "This last novel of Aldecoa's ... never seems to lift itself out of the clichés of its artificial plot, not [*sic*] to deepen its superficial views of Americans, who are portrayed largely as one-dimensional characters. Nor is the climax unexpected or thrilling; it is rather casual."[11] The author of these opinions overlooks the fact that Aldecoa's whole work is marked by a persistent and fruitful reevaluation of conventional narrative formulae, as is shown by the examples of "Young Sánchez," "Saint Eulalia of Steel," and many other stories.

The implied charge that the plot of *Part of a Story* is mediocre in conception and slack in execution cannot be sustained. The narrative is shaped with typical control and care. Climaxes are positioned in chapters 5 and 18, at symmetrical stages when approximately twenty and eighty percent of the narrative have elapsed. The prolongation of the action after Jerry's accidental death draws out the pain and agony felt not only by the *chonis*, islanders, and narrator, but also by the reader who is a compassionate spectator of the tragedy. Domingo Pérez Minik has described the effect of this controlled tempo as "cathartic."[12]

A sense of monotony and transience is fostered by the use of the continuous present tense. This transience is both a reflection of the natural environment in which the action takes place, and a condition of human life: "Yesterday was a day of great joy, today one of mourning. Life is like that" (181), it is said. Some instances of foreshadowing convey the inevitability of some fateful disaster. In chapter 12 El Fardelero "predicts that everything will end in a tragedy" (110), restating his conviction in the final sentence of the chapter. Jerry's death is prefigured in the grotesque mutilation of a dog in chapter 16, just four pages before he plunges into the sea, "chasing the reflection [of a comet] in the water, like a dog confused by someone's call" (172). This prophetic image is an example of the poetic coherence to be found in Aldecoa's most skillful narratives.

IV *Conclusion*

In *Part of a Story* Aldecoa consolidated his conception of the novel, as defined in *Great Sole*. Symbolism, metaphor, archetypal material, and organic duplication are the foundations of his art of fiction. He recognized the potential of "the sea novel," with its history of allegory and philosophical inquiry, for expressing moral and existential themes. *Part of a Story* is a restatement of his world view, as outlined in his second and third novels. Furthermore, it is a technical tour de force in which every procedure is dictated by theme. Aldecoa's tendency to reduce narrative action to a minimum culminates here. There is a renewed degree of refinement in his methods of suggestion and implication. And, as Charles Carlisle shows, he reaffirms his stylistic maturity in *Part of a Story*.[13]

CHAPTER 7

The Stories: Early Items and First Collections

I Early Stories

ALDECOA began to concentrate on writing narratives of short and intermediate length from the end of 1948. Most of these stories were brought together for publication in anthologies between 1955 and 1963, but Aldecoa chose to exclude from subsequent collections eleven early compositions written between 1948 and 1951. This was a matter of personal preference and not necessarily a reflection on his craft during that period. Though uneven in quality, these eleven stories deserve only slightly less attention than those of contemporaneous composition which were selected for reprinting.

Three of them: "La farándula de la media legua" ("The Half-league Drama Company"), "Función de aficionados" ("The Enthusiasts' Performance"), and "El teatro íntimo de doña Pom" ("Doña Pom's Private Theater") show the dismal fate of amateur dramatics in provincial society. While gently satirizing the cultural pretensions of the middle class, Aldecoa is attracted by the profitable theme of failure or frustrated ambition, also expressed in "El hombrecillo que nació para actor" ("The Little Man Who Was Born to Be an Actor"). "El loro antillano" ("The West Indian Parrot") and "El herbolario y las golondrinas" ("The Herbalist and the Swallows") are trivial in comparison. The first is a moderately funny sketch about a parrot which embarrasses its mistress by screeching left-wing slogans, and the second, a "considerably perverse" caricature of a cantankerous character, don Faustino.

"La fantasma de Treviño" ("The Ghost-Woman of Treviño") is interesting because of its disregard for verisimilitude. Another fantastic tale is the "Biografía de un mascarón de proa" ("A Biography of a Figurehead") which records the seafaring adventures of a personified figurehead, from its origins in a French wood until its destruction by fire. The story was deemed unsuitable for publication in the *Revista de Pedagogía* because it contained some offensive remarks about a priest. "La sombra del marinero que estuvo en Singapur" ("The Shadow of the Sailor who Visited Singapore") tells of the life and reminiscenses of a real sea dog. Aldecoa identifies romantically with Iñaqui, the nostalgic old sailor whose name is a popular Basque version of his own. Subsequent tales like "Rol del ocaso" ("Roll at Sunset"), "La noche de los grandes peces" ("The Night of the Big Fishes"), and the novel *Great Sole* are further expressions of his love of the sea.

The two remaining stories are somber in tone. "El ahogado" ("The Drowned Boy") describes the confusion and grief attendant on the post mortem of a child who drowns while playing near his school. In "Las miserias de un curandero" ("A Quack Doctor's Misfortunes") a superstitious farming community ostracizes a benevolent wise man who has failed to remedy a chronic drought. By strange coincidence, when he leaves the village a storm breaks and he is killed by lightning. According to its subtitle, the story is "a fable, but without a moral," and constitutes an attempt at allegory anticipating Aldecoa's intention in *Great Sole*. The thematic and technical variety of these narratives indicates Aldecoa's ambition to experiment with the potential of the short story medium, even if not to his own satisfaction.

II   Espera de tercera clase

This volume brings together ten stories originally published between 1950 and 1954, and confers a lasting corporate identity on them. *Espera de tercera clase* (*Waiting Room, Third Class*) opens with two stories in which the protagonists are children. "La humilde vida de Sebastián Zafra" ("The Humble Life of Sebastian Zafra") relates the childhood, adolescence, and maturity of a Gypsy, and "Chico de Madrid" ("The Kid from Madrid") describes the picaresque adventures and death of a thirteen-year-old beggar boy.

At the beginning of the first story, Sebastián Zafra has the appearance of an orphan. His mother died upon giving birth to him, and his father is constantly in and out of prison. However, he is cared for after a fashion by an aunt and uncle who live in squalor under a bridge on the city outskirts. Though timid in the presence of strangers, Sebastián leads a happy and adventurous life close to nature. We follow his personal development up to the time when he has married his cousin, Virtudes, and is awaiting the birth of their first child. One day he and his brother-in-law, the cautious and aptly named Prudencio, search an army training area for spent shells to sell as scrap metal. Sebastián carelessly touches an unexploded grenade which blows up, killing him and leaving Prudencio blind.

The plot of the second story, a biography in miniature, consists of a number of events significant in Chico's worldly education. He has learned about life the hard way. As a more or less innocent child he worked on a roundabout, hunted frogs and rats with a catapult, and idolized heroes of the screen such as Fu Man Chu. Exchanging the world of make-believe for that of fact, he switches his allegiance to a wily beggar and pickpocket who eventually gets him into trouble with the law. Chico recognizes the moral perfidy of his fellowman, and resolves to depend on no one other than himself. Some days later he goes exploring a sewer, but the adventure ends in disaster because he contracts typhoid and dies.

In both stories Aldecoa cultivates a narrative tone at once tender and ironic, occasionally even derisive. The innocence and joys of childhood, and the tragedy of premature death invite a lyrical treatment, but sentimentality has to be kept in check. So, a desire to disengage the reader's sympathy is apparent at the very beginning of "The Kid from Madrid," where the initial paragraph, with its tongue-in-cheek theorizing about techniques for tormenting animals, has a deliberately impersonal air. The tragicomic introduction of Chico is designed to fulfill a similar end. There are some truly poignant moments in Sebastián Zafra's life, for example, the occasion when he and the other "humble folk who live under the bridges"[1] visit his father in jail. But irony is just as efficient a means of arousing pity and fear for one who, as a Gypsy, leads a life of hardship and dies a gruesome death.

While similar in respect of plot, characterization, and narrative tone, the two stories differ in volume and proportions, and stylistic elaboration. The structure of "The Kid from Madrid," which defines the three major stages in Chico's apprenticeship to life, would seem out of proportion with a frame of only twenty-five hundred words. Sebastián Zafra's biography is contained in a more suitable form. The first story is also a more sophisticated artifact than the second. It exhibits some passages of patterned prose, with frequent reiteration of natural motifs, and instances of Aldecoa's favored technique of foreshadowing which reinforces the general sense of irony.

The aesthetic effect of "Hasta que llegan las doce" ("Waiting for Twelve O'Clock") rests on an ambiguity in the story's title which does not become apparent until the last half page. For little Juan Sánchez, an endearingly dreamy child from a working-class family, the period of free time allowed him by his mother will come to an end at midday. The narrative recounts Juan's earnest deliberations as to how he might best take advantage of this valuable hour or so. But it also happens that at a quarter to twelve his father, Pedro, is injured in an accident at a building site. There is a sudden variation in point of view and mood here, as the narrative voice becomes reticent and impassive. The story closes as it had begun, with an awesome image of factory sirens piercing the sky, suggesting the inevitable danger to which working men are exposed in an industrial environment.

"El aprendiz de cobrador" ("The Apprentice Conductor") treats of the single event which significantly alters the course of a person's life. Leocadio Varela has started work as a tram conductor, and punctuates professional routine with naive daydreams about Felisa, his fiancée. That July evening the couple celebrate Leocadio's first job with a group of friends in their neighborhood, and then go for a solitary walk along the road to Barajas. Leocadio's restlessness the following morning implies that he and Felisa have foresaken the innocence and freedom of youth, and must now face up to the responsibilities of adulthood.

Aldecoa presents this potentially dramatic situation in a deliberately low key, using a technique of insinuation. The narrative perspective shifts gradually from the impersonal public world, to the more familiiar *barrio* environment where Leocadio "becomes his usual self once more," and then to the sensual intimacy of the countryside, rich in wholesome aromas and animal sounds: "Leocadio feels a shiver run over his stomach. There's a fine breeze blowing. Felisa's eyes are black and shiny, like a beetle's wings" (I, 24). The style, previously direct and familiar, becomes refined and allusive at the delicate moment of impending sexual intimacy. In the concluding lines, metaphor and ambiguity convey Leocadio's mood of anxiety, as apparently innocent phrases from the introduction are suggestively repeated and acquire secretive, prophetic overtones. This tersely constructed story bears out one critic's impression of the genre, that "The reader must be able to look beyond the surface details, and perceive psychological development intuitively, without the need for explicit reference and description."[2]

The narrative of violence and delinquency is parodied in "Los atentados del barrio de la Cal" ("The Assaults in Lime Village"). The story describes the rivalry between two groups in a pathetic little neighborhood bathed in limestone dust. Differences of political opinion regularly lead Muñoz, who is "stupid, selfish, malevolent, and built like a heavyweight boxer," to clash with the supporters of Miguel, by contrast "a slim, good-natured [fellow]" (I, 225). This routine violence satisfies the popular need for excitement and gives the community something to talk about. Then one Saturday night, Muñoz suffers an unprecedentedly severe head injury, either at the hands of his rivals, who are lying in wait for him as usual, or as a result of his accidentally falling while on his drunken way home. This alarming incident actually serves to reconcile the two sides, putting an end to "the useless terrorism" in the neighborhood; as the narrator whimsically comments, the final assault turns out to be no less than "an act of Providence."

The caricaturesque opposition of Muñoz and Miguel, and the artificial conclusion illustrate the gusto with which Aldecoa presents this tale, subordinating realistic content to narrative artifice. The opening paragraph sets the tone, with an abundance of contradictory, incongruous, and exaggerated information about the neighborhood. Comic effect is sustained by the constant use of metaphor, syllepsis, chiasmus, and other rhetorical procedures. "The Assaults in Lime Village" represents the humorous alternative in Aldecoa's writing.

"Seguir de pobres" ("Continuing Poverty"), with which Aldecoa won the Youth Prize in 1953, demonstrates the centrality of human misfortune in his work. Five laborers converge on a small agricultural town looking for casual work at harvest time; one of them is stricken by a vicious brown wind, "el viento pardo," which wrecks both his health and his chances of successful employment. According to popular lore, the wind is symbolic of a menacing and destructive fate, connotations which Aldecoa also exploited in *With the East Wind.*

The ominous prominence accorded to "El Quinto" ("Number Five"), who is referred to as "un ser de silencio y de sombras"

("living in silence and shadows, I, 27), suggests that he is predes-
tined to a life of misfortune. In the terms of an image found in the
text, he is trapped like a fly in a spider's web. Social and political
factors have already left an indelible mark on him. "Number Five"
comes from a particularly poor area of Murcia, "where the people
bite their hands and weep, and everything is futile" (26). He found
himself on the losing side at the end of the Civil War, and has suffered imprisonment as a consequence. He also belongs to an underprivileged itinerant class, exploited by landowners and officialdom.
A farmer, Martín, who gives work to two of the group, San Juan
and Conejo, uses "a select, commercial vocabulary" to describe
the "material humano" ("hired hands") he has acquired. And the
mayor of the town dismisses Tito, Amadeo, and "Number Five" as
soon as the harvest is over, in spite of the fact that "Number Five"
is still weak and can barely walk, even with the aid of a stick.

   The song which Zito sings after their arrival at the town articulates the harvesters' discontent with their lot, and exposes social
injustice in an expressive antithesis: "Leaving for the harvest
makes a man feel sore. He works for the rich, but continues to be
poor" (30). The men's experience refutes official state propaganda
which shows healthy, contented farmhands earning handsome
sums of money with the honest sweat of their brow. Of course, the
narrator comments, these posters "don't mean a thing to the gangs
of harvesters who cross our cities, like a melancholy storm,
wandering all over the country in search of their daily bread" (25).
A bond of solidarity which develops between the five men is the
only heartening feature of this uncompromising, brooding tale,
which combines reflections on the human condition with revealing
criticism of socioeconomic hardship in postwar Spain.

   This sense of human defenselessness is compounded in "Muy de
mañana" ("Very Early in the Morning"). An old man's loneliness
becomes sadly complete when his only companion, a dog named
Cartucho, is run over by a car. Just before the accident Roque, a
melon vendor, had experienced a rare moment of happiness, think-
ing how well the fruit season had ended and how much he loved
and depended on Cartucho. The sudden twist in the plot points up
a powerful irony of fate. "Very Early in the Morning" is compact
and symmetrical in shape, and exhibits two stylistic hallmarks of
Aldecoa's writing: *iteratio* and sustained imagery.

   "Solar del Paraíso" ("Paradise Lot") is a reworking of the
Christian myth of man's expulsion from the Garden of Eden. In

this version, Pío Oliva's family is obliged to move on after their makeshift home, on a plot of land ironically known as "Paradise," has been destroyed by a freak storm. The owner of the site seizes this opportunity to remove his tenants, paying them off with a nominal sum in compensation. The promise of employment lures them to a work site some fifty kilometers away, at a place called La Cañada. Although the move represents material progress for the family — so much so that Pío's daughter-in-law, Agustina, refers to their new quarters as "a real paradise" — it is a spiritual fall from grace for Pío, who has been cast out of his normal environment into a world of solitude and confusion.

The first two sections of "Paradise Lot" contain numerous mythical elements. The story opens with an image of a "tumultuous, menacing river," which recalls biblical and Mesopotamian accounts of devastation by flood. In his description of the wasteland where Pío lives, the narrator makes a cutting remark about the owner, don Amadeo García, whose financial prosperity and physical bulk prevent him from passing through both the narrow door of "Paradise" and "the eye of the biblical needle." An inventory of the landscape also includes parodies of the Tree of Good and Evil, and the Wall of Sighs in Jerusalem. The words "cyclopean" and "titanism," which exaggerate the proportions of the tumbledown buildings in the lot, broaden the mythological terms of reference and anticipate the description of the thunderous storm as "titanic." This system of allusions brings out the enormity of man's material and psychological suffering in contemporary society. Aldecoa again points the finger at inadequate social and economic provisions, and identifies himself with those outcast and downtrodden groups whose situation is epitomized in the historic estrangement of the Jews.

The title phrase "A ti no te enterramos" ("We'll not See Your Funeral") figures in the next story as both a prophetic warning and a superfluous expression of encouragement to Valentín, a young man from a farming family who discovers he is suffering from tuberculosis. In the first of three chronological parts set in the months of June, March, and July respectively, Valentín worries about his health and considers moving to the city, where he imagines work will be plentiful and easier than in the country. He finally decides to leave after several months of forced inactivity have made him feel intolerably guilty about his uselessness on the farm. But conditions in the city are uncompromising and harsh, Valentín's

health goes from bad to worse, and after much soul-searching he
sees no alternative but to return home.

Aldecoa's study of moral responsibility against a silent background of anguish and conflict makes this story one of his most
satisfying from the psychological point of view. Valentín's mother
is a particularly felicitous creation. She has a perceptive understanding of the complex family drama and treats her husband and
sons with equal fairness. Her natural wisdom and uncomplicated
pragmatism are qualities subsequently handed on to Enedina in
Part of a Story.

"We'll not See Your Funeral" contains some descriptions of
natural scenery which rival those of Azorín for richness in sensuous
detail. But they capture the basic wholesomeness as well as the
conventional beauty of country life, and are meant to show how ill-
advised is Valentín's idea of leaving a natural setting for the
spurious attractions of city life. Elizabeth Espadas has praised the
originality of Aldecoa's "truthful and demythicized picture of
country life in twentieth-century Spain."[3] The same critic has analyzed aspects of Aldecoa's technique, for example, his ironic choice
of names which show up the family's desperate position. *Valiant*
though he may be, Valentín is doomed to die young; and his worn
out father, Salvador, is quite incapable of *saving* his family from
material hardship and spiritual suffering. The smallest of details is
thus seen to contribute to the story's single purpose.

The themes of urban destitution and death link "We'll not See
Your Funeral" to the following tale, "Quería dormir en paz" ("He
Only Wanted to Rest in Peace"). The central character, José Fernández Loinaga, is an especially pathetic example of the figure of
the victim often portrayed in Aldecoa's stories, for he suffers at the
hands of both society and fate. An unskilled laborer who has
known only slightly better times, José lives in a shanty town hovel,
where one of his small children is chronically sick. This early
morning he is detained by two policemen who find him asleep on a
park bench, without identity papers. At the police station José
explains, rather unconvincingly, that he has been unable to sleep at
home because of his son's illness. Two officers escort him there,
only to find that the child is dead, "resting in peace."

Our sympathy for the helpless underdog is educed as much by the
poignant tone of the narrative as by the unrelenting fatality of the
plot. Aldecoa makes characteristic use of understatement and other
rhetorical ploys, such as the reference to a pointedly ambivalent

clue in a police sergeant's crossword puzzle: the elusive word beginning with *h* and ending in *o* is most probably "hijo" ("son"), and the aim of this strategy is to indict official indifference to José's personal tragedy. "He Only Wanted to Rest in Peace" is a most touching account of human misfortune, and a keen exposure of urban poverty.

III Vísperas del silencio

Vísperas del silencio (*The Eve of Silence*) includes five narratives of intermediate length. In the title story Aldecoa adopts a technique of sustained antithesis to repudiate class inequality and denounce bourgeois values and habits. There are two alternating strands in the plot of "The Eve of Silence" which juxtapose the moral dissolution of a well-to-do household with the physical disintegration of a working-class family in Madrid. César Yustas cleans out the city's drains, amid "rats, filth and darkness," and lives in an attic with his long-suffering wife, Pilar, and their three sons. Little Paquito dies of a prolonged bronchial condition, and some weeks later Mariano, the eldest brother, turns professional with a third division football team; Victor, an apprentice mechanic, remains with his parents in their shabby home. Meanwhile, in another household, don Orlando Salvador de la Maza pursues some illegal business interests which enable him to live comfortably with his troublesome family. Rafael, a lazy and irresponsible youth, tries unsuccessfully to elope with his girlfriend, Teresa; and Mercedes, whose sickly child, Fonchi, is the cause of much concern to Orlando, treats her weak-willed husband, Crisanto, with increasing coldness and disdain. The relation of one story line to another is strengthened by a number of analogies. For example, in each family there is a sick child and a wayward teenage son; both Paquito and Crisanto are fond of drawing and painting; and Pilar and Mercedes appear sewing in consecutive passages of part one.

Notwithstanding Aldecoa's claim that his attitude to social issues was "neither sentimental nor tendentious,"[4] his contrastive argument is blatantly one-sided here. Orlando and his children are weak, intolerant, greedy, or selfish; the members of César's family possess spiritual qualities which amply compensate for their material poverty. Paquito is a courageous, good-natured child, and Mariano shows much affection for his parents. Images of putrefaction emphasize the decadence of bourgeois morals. César may work in filthy, obnoxious surroundings, but the human atmosphere in Orlando's household is "rotten" — an adjective which Crisanto also uses to describe the company his wife keeps. When César and Municio emerge from a foul-smelling drain, the fresh air gives them nausea; yet even the atmosphere of his country farm cannot cure the sickness in Orlando's soul. A rotten ball of wool which the innocent Paquito sees lying in the gutter is another image of this corruption.

Besides portraying the contrary fortunes of two families, the story also presents a panoramic tableau of Madrid in the postwar period. Madrid is seen as a city of death and corruption. The Civil War is recalled in the words of a publican who asks César whether there is any truth in the rumor that a soldier's corpse has been found in the sewers. The action is set during autumn and winter, thus symbolizing a process of decline. In the final section Aldecoa describes Madrid in the grip of silence and darkness, and anticipates the dawning of a new day when "Life will go on; life with its tales of hope, joy, grief, and suffering. . ." (II, 96).

"Santa Olaja de acero" ("Saint Eulalia of Steel") tells of a representative day in the life of Higinio, a railway man who drives an engine of that name. In the first part Higinio leaves his sleeping wife, meets his stoker, Mendaña, at the yard, and together they set off with a heavy load of freight. The action of the second part is situated in mountainous country, where the train threatens to run out of control as it descends a steep incline. Higinio barely manages to prevent an accident between his own and an approaching passenger train just a few kilometers down the track. In the final part it is night time; the two men finish work and, as they take a drink with some other drivers, joke uneasily about their "miraculous" escape. After complaining about the awkward hours he has to work, Higinio leaves Mendaña and goes home to his wife, whom he finds asleep in bed virtually as he had left her that morning.

The story is a masterpiece of arrangement, opening and closing with a description of a darkened room, in which the principal motifs are repeated precisely. As James Abbott has noted, this symmetry isolates the events of one day in such a way that "Aldecoa depicts, symbolically, the traveler's journey through life."[5] The hermetic framework also suggests the exploited worker's imprisonment in a limited world. Aldecoa discerns the epic potential in a humble profession which involves hardship and danger, and imbues his story with a warm spirit of solidarity. The intimate introductory paragraph engages the reader's sympathy for the unassuming driver who, when subsequently confronted with a critical situation, shows an exemplary degree of courage and equanimity. A common bond links Higinio and Mendaña together, and they in turn identify closely with their locomotive, personifying it affectionately: "Eulalia was the head, the intellect, the source of energy for that train, which had taken on a human appearance for them" (II, 19).

Concerning the plot, the men's narrow escape from a collision with another train is an extraordinary incident, but Aldecoa deprives this crucial event of an abrupt climax and dramatic result, in a deliberate deformation of the conventional plot. This practice, resumed in later stories, is an example of the author's constant search for a viable alternative to the well-made, eventful story line which Azorín, André Gide, and Virginia Woolf had regarded as an anachronism half a century or so before. Variation of rhythm and tone is employed to complement this vestigial action. A uniform tempo is slowly established and events accelerate to an imminent climax; the narrative then resumes a normal pace, finally decelerating in the last four paragraphs. The tone alters significantly at the beginning of the crucial second part, where the narrator dwells on the menacing properties of railway tunnels. When the train enters the mountains, Higinio's remark, that "The sleepers are half rotten. One of these days we'll topple down, and take all the goods with us" (16), ominously foreshadows the drama of the runaway train, which is in fact prompted by an obstruction of the line where some sleepers are being replaced.

Aldecoa's narrative technique is restrained, as befits the mood of subdued heroism. In the passage describing the crisis, he equals Kafka's ability to create and prolong, but also to contain, tension. The deliberate understatement with which the second part concludes highlights indirectly the truly perilous nature of the situation. The laconic dialogue at the end of the narrative also illustrates this sober technique of allusion: " 'Hello, Higinio,' his wife said in a hoarse, sleepy voice. 'How did it go today?' Higinio answered, 'Okay. The same as usual' " (24). Although there are some passages containing imagery and sensuous descriptions of nature, the style is plainer here than in many other stories of the period.

The earliest of the tales included in *The Eve of Silence* is "Los vecinos del callejón de Andín" ("The Folk from Andin Lane"). This story relates the experience of a small group of people in a cul-de-sac community between 24 November and 1 January of an unspecified year. Part 1 humorously describes the possibility of conflict on two levels: the malevolent watchmaker bears a portentous grudge against Bayoneta, his daughter's ne'er-do-well fiancé; and the remarkable Panchito (a habitual drunkard) is involved in some dealings with stolen goods. The narrative of part 2 first mentions Paca Martínez's brothel, then focusses on the tavern where a suspicious event, probably related to crime, is the topic of conversation, and concludes with a scuffle between Antonio, Paca's son, and Bayoneta. Antonio has been provoked by the watchmaker into assaulting Bayoneta, but retires in defeat after receiving a minor wound, apparently from his opponent's razor. In part 3 the innkeeper discovers that Antonio was in fact cut by a piece of glass lying on the ground, and Paca, furious at the thought that the watchmaker made her son risk his life, recovers her good humor over a glass of beer. A mad dog strays into the alley and is shot by two timorous policemen who Panchito quite wrongly fears have come to arrest him. Peace having been restored, the third part ends with the news that the authorities have ordered the closure of doña Paca's brothel. The action of part 4 takes place some weeks later when the inhabitants of the lane hold a New Year's party, a joyous occasion on which old grievances are forgotten and friendships renewed. Panchito is finally imprisoned, and the culminating event is the installation of a urinal in the cul-de-sac by the authorities.

The prefatory gloss, "A well-meaning, if silly tale," anticipates the prevailing sense of comedy and exaggeration in "The Folk from Andin Lane." The first piece of narrative information is that undiscriminating drunks use the lane as a place for relieving themselves. This detail reappears with comic insistence throughout the tale. Bathos and melodrama pervade that part of the action involving Antonio, who suffers a triple reversal in his dramatic fortune: his show of bravado gives way to tremulous cowardice when he confronts Bayoneta; he suffers the humiliation of defeat; and his "wound" turns out to be no more than a scratch. The section which relates these melodramatic events bears the appropriate heading: "Here: how tempers flared but nothing happened" (II, 168).

The use of such headings entails mimicry of a device used in classical texts such as *El Conde Lucanor* and *Don Quixote*. It is but one instance of Aldecoa's recourse to parody and burlesque in

"The Folk from Andin Lane." The author deliberately apes the conventions of the dramatic tale of jealousy and passion, and the heroic mode of the epic. Antonio abandons a hysterical Cecilia "in a theatrical scene" and leaves the brothel in full cry, "just like the knights must have set out on their crusades." His challenge to Bayoneta incorporates a well-worn phrase, "There's not enough room for two of us in this town," which, as the narrator remarks, Antonio "remembered from a show" (166). When the victorious Bayoneta runs away after the fight, he receives "two hearty blows from the night watchman, who handled his baton like the Cid wielded his sword" (167). The effect of these techniques of inflation and deflation is in part to ridicule the character's pretentious and absurd behavior, but Aldecoa's ultimate aim is to redeem from oblivion those who lead insignificant lives.

"El mercado" ("The Market") resembles "The Eve of Silence" in many fundamental respects. It deals with the tenuously connected financial affairs of two families, and counterpoints the disproportionate fortunes and values of the proletariat and bourgeoisie. Florencio Ruiz collects refuse with the assistance of his wife and niece, and earns some extra money through the illegal sale of lead piping and other materials. Don Matías Cerro, married to his second wife Leonor, and father of José María, Leonorcita, and the retarded Pedrolas, conducts some shady business deals, selling fish no longer fresh. Antonio, Leonorcita's fiancé, provides the link between the two groups, for it is he who buys the stolen goods from Florencio.

Aldecoa's passionate concern for the exploited refuse collectors is immediately visible. In the introduction Florencio, Dolores, and Julita emerge from a symbolically oppressive landscape "into the dreary light, a dirty shade of blue." The metonymical reference to "dust carts," instead of direct allusion to the people themselves, conveys a gloomy impression of reification. Aldecoa's description of the two women, "[their] faces like earth, furrowed faces with big, staring eyes which seemed to be witnessing something cruel" (II, 181), recalls the sinister naturalist emphasis on environmental, and especially telluric, determinism.

The characteristic attitudes of both parties are shrewdly portrayed. Dolores and Julita gauge wealth and status by the quality of refuse families leave to be collected: "Hey Auntie, have you seen this? A tin with a label in English or something like that. I bet these people really live it up" (183). Florencio finds it quite understandable that Julita should have acquired "an occasional husband" while Remedios was in prison. The question of sexual conduct is viewed quite differently in the bourgeois code. Don Matías "keeps a mistress in an out-of-the-way apartment fitted with all modern conveniences" (187); and Leonor demands the immediate marriage of her daughter and Antonio when she suspects them of a prematurely advanced degree of intimacy. The typifying characteristics of bourgeois morality, as depicted here, are pretense and artificiality. Leonor behaves in a "theatrical," "spectacular" fashion, and is in her element when she can show off her best china — "for use on special occasions" — and fuss over a new dress bought for Leonorcita's wedding. She is concerned primarily with appearances and is determined to make the neighbors green with envy, by organizing an impressive social event. This materialistic attitude is celebrated in the story's title, indicative, at one level, of the commercial basis of social relations.

The plot incorporates elements of crime, intrigue, and romance. Julita's lover, Esteban, disappears with most of the money Florencio had made through selling stolen lead; the male characters conduct their shady business deals in an atmosphere of exaggerated secrecy; Julita and Remedios are reconciled, although Reme suffers a degrading beating from Esteban; and Antonio marries Leonorcita in a pompous and vulgar ceremony. The action extends over a period of several weeks, and the nine sections of the narrative isolate those moments particularly illustrative of social values or crucial in the development of the plot. The part of the story relating to the Cerros has a conventional ending; in the other, Remedios becomes conscious of his responsibility and proudly takes Florencio's place on the cart. Since Florencio had followed a similar path when he was a young man, Aldecoa appears to be suggesting that the fortunes and experience of these exploited people take the form of a recurrent cyclical process.

The narrative is constructed with calculated precision as regards both the release of information and the juxtaposition of scenes. At the beginning of chapter 3 the narrator accords no apparent importance to the fact that Matías has a mistress, but concludes the chapter with a mischievously significant remark: "He knew perfectly well where he was going to spend the rest of the evening. He stopped at a sweetshop to buy a box of chocolates. Matías wore his hat slightly tilted to one side in a cocky and derisive attitude" (193). When Florencio asks his wife if their recent earnings are hidden in a safe place, his anxiety prepares the reader for the discovery that Esteban has stolen most of the money. And Matías' interest in the page of the newspaper reporting "the fines imposed by the tax office" (222) is a succinct reminder of his illegal activities. Structural counterpoint and montage are used for particularly ironic effect in chapter 5. Here, Antonio's father reminds him of the financial advantage to be gained by marrying Leonorcita, while in a similar conversation Matías tells his wife: "An ambitious fellow, that Antonio. I think he's pretty well off. We'll have to let our daughter go and not miss this opportunity" (204).

Aldecoa's view of humanity and society is at its most ironic here. A particularly interesting example of his attitude to human foibles, irrespective of any class distinction, is the episode in which Remedios and Julita see a film about the heroic return of a soldier from the war and his romantic reconciliation with his wife, a deliberate parody of their own troubled experience. Interior duplication, more frequent in the novels than the stories, is a telling means of differentiating between naive imagination and harsh reality.

The commonplace in life provides the subject matter of "El autobús de las 7:40" ("The Bus at 7:40"), for which a possible source is Steinbeck's *The Wayward Bus*. The first half of the story introduces six characters waiting at a tavern for the morning bus to Madrid. They include Sebastián, a soldier on leave, two prostitutes called Concha and Luisa, a child on his way to school, a professional gentleman, don Joaquín, and a respectable lady from the middle class. Their small talk and unexceptional private thoughts, together with detailed attention to the physical setting, make up the narrative. Aldecoa portrays the subtle yet familiar mechanism of human behavior and social interaction. For instance, the prostitutes provoke and embarrass Sebastián, who is relieved to acquire some moral support from the innkeeper; and Joaquín, who had actually been with Concha and Luisa the previous evening, now pretends he does not know them, uneasily maintaining the pretense as he discusses the morals of society with the lady in black. There follows an extensive section of psychological analysis, with virtually no reference to external factors such as the progress of the journey, which serves merely as a framework allowing the author to penetrate the passengers' minds at length. He shows Sebastián's frustration and lack of confidence with the opposite sex, Concha's earthy but romantic thoughts about her absent lover, Luisa's venomous, defensive reaction to the lady in black, Joaquín's fascination with them both and his concealed disdain for the middle-class lady, the latter's self-righteous indignation at Concha and Luisa's presence, and the schoolboy's distractions and reluctant anticipation of the day's lessons: "As soon as they reached the village he'd have to get off the bus and wearily make his way to the poor, broken-down, disagreeable school, where he'd be taught something of no particular interest but which he'd have to explain a few moments later" (I, 249).

With the schoolboy's departure the hermetic quality of the central section is interrupted, and the narrative tempo accelerates as the bus enters Madrid. The human relations established during the trip reach an awkward conclusion when Concha exposes Joaquín's hypocrisy with a calculated verbal indiscretion which mortally offends the lady in black and gives the two women the satisfaction of having dealt the last blow. The soldier, as indecisive as ever, fails in his plan to approach Concha and Luisa and is left in pathetic isolation, as at the beginning of the story.

"The Bus at 7:40" exemplifies the transformed costumbrist element in Aldecoa's work. It was his ambition to depict the "harsh but appealing reality of Spain" in the 1950s,[6] and he does so with intimate fidelity, transcending both the sentimental naivety of Fernán Caballero and the grotesque vision often present in Camilo José Cela's *Apuntes carpetovetónicos* (*Sketches of the Heart of Castile*). The influence of *Viaje a la Alcarria* (*Journey to the Alcarria*) must not be underestimated, however, for in that work Cela also accounts with alternating tenderness and crudeness for the social reality of provincial Spain. In Aldecoa's tale the bus journey is important only as a representative event, and the characters, though all endowed with distinctive individual traits, function as a typical social group. Also treated is the theme of the contrast between rural and urban society, a consistent feature of the new costumbrist literature. Apart from these issues, the reader is impressed by the author's concern for humanity, especially noticeable in the sympathetic presentation of the child and in the determined, but in no way vicious, censure of hypocrisy and prejudice.

IV   Two Early Volumes of Stories: a Conclusion

The reader of *Waiting Room, Third Class* and *The Eve of Silence* may remark on Aldecoa's self-assured mastery of the genre, as did his commentators in 1955. Mariano Tudela celebrated the publication of these two volumes with the assurance that their author would come to occupy "a unique place in the history of our literature."[7] Aldecoa's work evinces sensitivity and insight into subtle aspects of human psychology, and an ability to portray the emotional and intellectual processes of people from many walks of life. Although inspired by routine aspects of existence, Aldecoa also wrote about the extraordinary event and its effect on a person's life. The well-to-do appear in his stories, but only as a term of critical comparison with the humble and underprivileged who are his main concern. While his art has a firm moral intention, there is no didacticism in his treatment of man's hypocrisy and egoism, or of social inequality and injustice. His view of mankind is shot through with humor, irony, and, in the words of Ramón de Garciasol, "a certain mood of overall pessimism"[8] concerning the role of fate and the preponderance of conflict in human experience.

The plots of Aldecoa's stories often have dramatic potential which is played down suggestively in tales like "Waiting for Twelve O'Clock" and "Saint Eulalia of Steel." Signs of the same dissatisfaction with accepted literary modes are visible in Aldecoa's parodies of typecast plots. As regards narrative technique, the author generally prefers understatement and concise allusion to a more direct manner of presentation; illustrations may be found in the abrupt and enigmatic introductions of "He Only Wanted to Rest in Peace" and "The Eve of Silence," and the use of suspended points toward the close of "The Apprentice Conductor" and in "The Humble Life of Sebastian Zafra." On considering Aldecoa's accommodation to the technical demands of the short story, we note a greater degree of involvement and identification with his characters than is shown in the novels.

Formal devices are exploited to fulfill a poetic function. The alternation between passages of monologue and narrative in "We'll not See Your Funeral" and "Paradise Lot," and the cyclical narrative of "The Apprentice Conductor" evoke moods of despair or unrest. The juxtaposition of the affairs of two families of different social standing in "The Market" is a similar instance of symbolic form.

Aldecoa's prose style is rich in imagery. There are symbolic objects like the spider's web in "Continuing Poverty" or the broken jug in "Paradise Lot." Imagery is sometimes sustained throughout a story, as in "We'll not See Your Funeral" where a picture of the moon is a *memento mori,* a frightening reminder of

Valentín's tuberculous condition. In systematic application, imagery may serve as a metaphorical extension of the theme, as in "The Eve of Silence." And it can define a character with ironic force when used in names like Piorrea — the toothpaste salesman in "The Folk from Andin Lane" — or Pío — the outcast from paradise in "Paradise Lot." Aldecoa's style is sometimes conceptually baroque in a manner reminiscent of Quevedo and Gómez de la Serna. It also abounds in devices such as transferred epithets, *iteratio,* and multiple series of words frequently in a relation of syllepsis or oxymoron. From the start of his career Aldecoa acquired the reputation of being a master of style.

CHAPTER 8

Two Further Volumes of Stories

I   El corazón y otros frutos amargos

P UBLISHED in 1959, *El corazón y otros frutos amargos* (*The Heart and Other Bitter Fruits*) contains ten stories already printed in newspapers and journals between 1953 and 1957, and one new creation which lends its name to the collection. There is a uniformity of tone which leaves the reader with an impression of melancholy and despair. We can dispense with analyses of the following four stories: "La urraca cruza la carretera" ("The Magpie Flies Over the Road"), because it repeats the theme of the uneven distribution of wealth; "Rol del ocaso" ("Westward Roll"), because it closely resembles *Great Sole* in the shape and rhythm of plot and in narrative presentation; "Entre el cielo y el mar" ("Between the Sky and the Sea"), because it does not represent the best in Aldecoa's stories of the sea; and "Esperando el otoño" ("Waiting for Autumn"), because it is vitiated by the very quality of boredom which it is meant to describe.

Though on a proportionally smaller scale, "En el kilómetro 400" ("At the 400 Kilometer Mark") is similar to *Blood and Lightning* and *Great Sole* in narrative shape and tempo. The story charts the slow progress of two lorries transporting fish from Pasajes in the north of Spain to Madrid, by enumerating place-names along the route: Vitoria, Aranda de Duero, Somosierra, and others. Having fallen behind their mates Iñaqui and Martiricorena, the drivers Severiano and Luisón later come across their overturned truck some distance outside Madrid. An urgent change of rhythm at this point conveys the men's anxiety to reach the hospital where Martiricorena has been taken with serious injuries.

Aldecoa's strategy for involving the reader is much the same as in *Great Sole*. While working to establish a sense of monotony in the first three quarters of the story, he also resorts to a number of dis-

109

turbing and subversive devices. In the opening scene Luisón is
shown reading a cowboy comic carrying the usual emphasis on danger and death. Then, Severiano and Luisón casually exchange some
words of caution about the mechanical safety of their truck. It is
suggested that Martiricorena — the first part of whose name means
"Martyr" — is unreliable at the wheel; like Simón Orozco he is due
for retirement. The comic interlude in a café-bar run by a testy
character called Salvador is another technical success. Premonitions and contrasts such as these are the key to the narrative
mechanism. They provide the muted tension indispensable to
drama, and convey the inevitability of misfortune in the lives of
men who, like Higinio and Mendaña in "Saint Eulalia of Steel,"
are obliged to court danger in their work every day.

    This dramatic effect is also achieved through a contrast in styles.
There is a wealth of narrative, descriptive, and psychological detail
in the opening section, and recourse to patterning in the sequences
which relate the lorry's progress. The atmosphere of nighttime is
evoked in the third paragraph by reference to the various noises
made by frightened animals — frogs, owls, foxes — as the traffic
passes them by. By contrast, "At the 400 Kilometer Mark" closes
with a passage of abrupt dialogue and the tense remark that
"Luisón and Severiano did not speak. Luisón and Severiano had
their eyes on the road" (I, 88).

    "Young Sánchez," like *Neutral Corner,* is the fruit of Aldecoa's
identification with the heroic and primitive world of boxing. While
the motto from a poem by Vachel Lindsay might suggest a literary
basis to his interest, it must be remembered that Aldecoa cultivated
a firsthand acquaintance with this peculiar environment. His
stories portray the blood, sweat, and hardship of a crude world
bearing little resemblance to the spectacular image of the big time.
The opening section of "Young Sánchez" captures the unique
flavor and atmosphere of gymnasia where aspiring boxers train for
a hard-earned fight. Conditions are sordid, the air salty and dank
"like a soiled towel." Would-be champions must take some
ungratifying job to finance their training and buy equipment.
Paco, alias "Young," Sánchez has at last secured his first professional fight, against a hard-hitting and experienced boxer called
Bustamante. The story traces his steady preparation over the fort-
night leading up to the contest, and stops short at the moment the
bell sounds and fighting is about to begin.

    As a narrative, "Young Sánchez" is interesting because of the way it flaunts the reader's expectations. An exciting climax is promised throughout the story's twenty-nine pages, only to be denied in an abrupt, suspenseful conclusion. The accepted relation between development and solution is deliberately upset here, and the reader is forced to admit that what matters in the story is the quality of the human experience it portrays, and not the extent to which it conforms to any narrative paradigm.

"Young Sánchez" is an exemplary study of human sensibility. Paco's character illustrates a mild form of *machismo* which is not in the least objectionable if compared with the conduct of Sebastián Vázquez at the beginning of *With the East Wind*. Paco wears his hair long with one greasy lock falling over his forehead, and vainly displays his hairy chest. An element of presumption is visible in the way he treats his servile sister and idolizing father, and in the pleasure he derives from being a local sporting hero. He is vulnerable and sensitive, however, as the confusing interview with his promoter shows. And he is stricken by fear while waiting in the dressing room before his fight with Bustamante. As the bell sounds for the contest to begin, Paco sees that he is not fighting for himself after all, but for his long-suffering family and their redemption. The story need proceed no further than the revelation of this simple human truth.

The absurdity of society's behavior and values is exposed in "Un cuento de reyes" ("A Christmas Tale"), as Aldecoa engineers an arbitrary improvement in the protagonist's fortunes. Omicrón Rodríguez, a humble, good-natured and exceedingly ugly Negro, works as a casual photographer in the streets of Madrid, earning barely enough to survive. His luck takes an unexpected turn for the better when a complete stranger offers him a considerable sum of money to play the part of Balthazar in a Christmas procession. Omicrón's outstanding success in the fictitious role of black king shows up the fickleness of a society which one day condemns a man for the color of his skin and the next singles him out for temporary celebrity. With this *volte face*, habitual roles are ironically reversed as people lining the street clamor to take Omicrón's photograph; one spectator even asks if he is really black. Doses of dry humor thus reinforce the critical intention of this tale.

Alicia Bleiberg's classification of "Al otro lado" ("Over on the Other Side") and "Tras de la última parada" ("Beyond the End of the Line") as stories concerning "emigration from the countryside into the city"[1] is not strictly correct, for the theme of "Beyond the

End of the Line" is that of national emigration from Spain which Lauro Olmo dramatized skillfully in his play *La camisa* (*The Shirt,* 1962). What does link the two stories is their common mood of discontent with the human cost, in terms of instability and alienation, of an inadequate socioeconomic system. The characters' alienation goes beyond the mere physical segregation or neglect depicted in the local imagery of both titles.

In the first story material hardship is illustrated by the appalling conditions in which Martín Jurado lives with his family, in one of a vast and unseemly colony of shacks put together with broken tiles, slates, pieces of tin, and other discarded materials. But it is the spiritual toll of displacement which weighs most heavily. Protracted unemployment has forced Martín into such a position that he will soon have no alternative but to go begging, an affront to his dignity which he cannot tolerate. In "Beyond the End of the Line" Mercedes Gomera Ruiz may avail herself of the opportunity to emigrate, but only at the risk of sacrificing family unity.

"Over on the Other Side" is as uncompromising in its denunciation as "Continuing Poverty" from the previous volume. The author explains how Martín had first come to the city in the naive hope of finding wealth and happiness, only to find that outsiders like himself are the last to be catered for. Their position is resumed in a stark chiasmus: "Ellos están fuera de la ciudad, la ciudad tiene fronteras con ellos" ("They are outside the city, the city has boundaries with them," I, 280). "Beyond the End of the Line" is a story of greater technical subtlety, for the reader is drawn into identifying with an anonymous bureaucrat, "el hombre de la ciudad" ("the man from the city"), whose duty is to inform Mercedes Gomera that she has permission to leave Spain. His visit to the humble rooms which Mercedes shares with her invalid father affects him profoundly, and the sympathetic reader cannot but share his feelings of guilt and unrest. Carmen Martín Gaite has similar recourse to a sensitive intermediary of this type in her persuasive moral story, "La conciencia tranquila" ("The Untroubled Conscience").

"Los hombres del amanecer" ("The Early Risers") introduces two old men, Lino and Cristobal, who make a living by catching vipers for scientific experiments. Amusing though their eccentricity may be, it implies an offense against human dignity and is fraught with danger to life and health. Aldecoa does not flinch from depicting an infrareality which has its literary origins in the naturalist and tremendist views. His work is neverless closer to the first school in tone and attitude. The story is designed to shock the reader with two revelations, at the halfway point and near the conclusion. In the first instance we learn just what it is that the men are hunting, and in the second, we share Lino's disappointment and ironical disgust that don Rafael, the scientist, now wants large quantities of rats, not vipers, for his laboratory.

"The Heart and Other Bitter Fruits" sets an imposing seal on this collection of stories. It combines remarkable sensitivity to human feelings with profound social concern. In Juan Montilla López, Aldecoa has created a memorable character whose unrefined emotions and reactions make him a lifelike individual. From his bewildered arrival at a desolate country town where he finds temporary work as a farm laborer, until his bewildering premature departure only two days later, he captures the reader's attention with his overall susceptibility. His moods of embarrassment and timidity, of impatience and jealousy, are convincingly portrayed in conversations with the owner of the farm, a laborer called Rogelio, and María, the kitchen maid. Juan would dearly like to say gallant things to María, but can never find the right words when the opportunity arises.

If Juan's shifting relations with Rogelio, María, and her hale partner, *Rediez*, occupy the foreground of "The Heart and Other Bitter Fruits," a broader pattern of social consequences looms in the background. For Juan is an emigrant inside his own country. His situation, like that of the itinerant workers in "Continuing Poverty," shows up a flaw in the whole social organism of postwar Spain. He represents all those who "suffer the changes, the perplexity of the unknown..." (I, 89), and are haunted by nostalgia for their *patria chica* ("home country").

For the most part, Aldecoa adopts an objective mode of narrative presentation, but occasional shifts to a subjective angle lay bare the intimate workings of Juan Montilla's mind. A short passage of interior monologue, as he drives a mule-drawn cart across the fields, brings out his sense of disappointment at having failed to impress María, and the subconscious fear that he may have made a fool of himself. There are no such glimpses into Juan's mind in the final pages, where the narrative is restrained and antirhetorical. Each reader is left to infer from Juan's remote behavior the motives behind his decision to leave with Rogelio and *Rediez*. The

few words he utters signal some kind of emotional upheaval which
remains unexplained.

Stylistic effects are functional and precise. The duplication of
verbs and adverbs in the opening paragraph conveys a mood of
lethargic uncertainty which is to permeate the entire story. Imagery
is used to suggest ideas and feelings which would be debased by
denotation or definition. So, Juan Montilla's diffidence is conveyed in a passage which contrasts the stumbling of submissive
mules with the indomitable fury of a bull, which to Juan's mind
symbolizes a man's self respect. And the hoopoe bird that flies
overhead as Juan and his two companions approach the railway
station represents the impermanence and oblivion to which all itin-
erants are condemned, for it is a bird which removes all traces of
human presence by wiping out footprints along the road.

In his review of the volume *The Heart and Other Bitter Fruits,*
José Ramón Marra López declared Aldecoa "an undisputed master
of the short story," and continued: "No one else knows how to use
language with quite such wisdom and mastery as a means to exploit
the vein of tender and poignant, bitter and grayish poetry which lies
concealed in reality.... A short story [by Aldecoa] gives the
impression of something complete, perfectly constructed, and
packed with all the possibilities of drama or irony."[2] The next
volume of stories continues to justify Marra López's enthusiasm.

II Caballo de pica

The title story of *Caballo de pica* (*The Picador's Mount*) stands
loosely as a model, in theme and mood, for some of the other
narratives in the collection. Aldecoa takes the bullring to symbolize
the human world of social relations, and singles out the igno-
minious function of the horses ridden by *picadores* in the second
stage of a *corrida* when the bull is goaded. The horses are exposed
to a physical onslaught which may end in fatal injury, but there is
no appreciation of their role, no acknowledgment of their suffering. They symbolize people who are quite simply exploited as
instruments and treated no better than animals. This symbolism is
indicated clearly in "The Picador's Mount" which focuses on a
central character, Pepe el Trepa, an ex-bullfighter, now friendless,
sick, and poor at the age of fifty-seven. Pepe curries favor with
Juan Rodrigo but has to suffer humiliation and abuse for the privilege of his company. One night Juan invites him to join a group of

friends in drink and song. Pepe's inability to keep up with the younger, healthier drinkers annoys a malicious one among them, who forces a funnel down Pepe's throat and pours so much wine into it that he chokes to death. Juan had first introduced Pepe to the group as "ese jamelgo que no le quieren ya ni para la pica" ("the old nag they don't even want for the picador's mount," 1, 123). He is again compared with a horse as he kicks and splutters in protest and when he lies inert on the tavern floor. The comparison operates both as an element in the story's rhetoric of horror and as a comment on the hapless condition of those whom society has discarded.

The pitch of disaster reached here is not equaled in any of the remaining stories, nor are the roles of outcast and victim combined again so forcefully. Rather, the *dramatis personae* of the volume consist of those who live in an inhospitable environment or enjoy only marginal status, and whose suffering or sudden misfortune stops short of catastrophe. Running through many of the stories is the sense that man's life is a spiritual exile and a state of incompleteness. A line from the work of Antonio Machado prefaces the volume: "Y cuanto exilio en la presencia cabe" ("And how much exile there is in existence"). "La tierra de nadie" ("No Man's Land"), a story about a young soldier on military service far from his native soil, is an example. Lying face down on the ground of a disused airfield, the young man is filled with nostalgia for the familiar aromas of his rural background. His lack of feeling for the suburban landscape is a reaction common to those affected by the destruction of the environment. As city boundaries encroach on the countryside, the ties between man and nature are severed and the land loses its character and appeal. The title phrase, "No Man's Land," is thus given a multiple significance beyond conventional usage.

This sense of incompatibility with one's surroundings and mood of spiritual unrest are expressed in three other stories. In "El porvenir no es tan negro" ("The Future is not so Gloomy"), Miss Sánchez is the odd one out in a group of middle-aged office employees. Scenes and conversations from family life at the home of one of her happily married colleagues throw into relief her tragic inadequacy as a frustrated spinster. Luisa, one of two sisters described in "Dos corazones y una sombra" ("Two Hearts and One Shadow"), is also painfully out of place. On the particular day in question it is her turn to do the household chores and, in the evening, to retire to

her room alone while her sister, Carmen, receives the attentions of
Jaime, the suitor they share on an alternating basis. In this unique
ménage à trois Luisa can look forward to the following day with a
paradoxical mixture of pleasure and disgust. The aptly titled
"Fuera de juego" ("Offside") is the third story in this group.
Here, Pablo, black sheep in a bourgeois family, rebels against the
prevailing ethos of "social standing, wealth, respectability, and vir-
tuous ways" (I, 178). His attitude provokes unpleasantness and
isolates him from the rest of the family.

The Two stories are inspired by the contemplation of routine suffering. The distraught woman who consults a spiritualist in "Her-
mana Candelas" ("Sister Candelas"), and the pompous mayor
who wages a ridiculous war against public indecency in "La espada
encendida" ("The Burning Sword") both bear the terrible cross of
loneliness. The woman, abandoned in love, is desperate for com-
forting advice. The mayor's crusading zeal in matters of civic
morality is meant to compensate for the emptiness of his private
life. Still in mourning for his wife, he dreads having to return to an
empty house and invents schemes to keep himself busy outside normal working hours. He gains our heartfelt sympathy, in spite of
being the butt of Aldecoa's habitual jibes at authority. Greater
emphasis on action in the plots of "La despedida" ("The Leave
Taking") and "Aunque no haya visto el sol" ("Even Though He
May Not Have Seen the Sun") entails a more dramatic treatment of
the same theme of loneliness. The fact that the victim of sudden
misfortune is in the first case sick and old, and in the second, blind
and downtrodden, increases the quality of pathos in these two
pieces.

The remaining four stories do not readily match any of the types
differentiated so far. "Balada del Manzanares" ("Ballad of the
River Manzanares") is a narrative of great poetic and dramatic
intensity, with none of the melancholic emotive undertones of, for
example, "The Leave Taking." A potentially gloomy theme, that
of working conditions in urban industry, is passed over summarily
so that the author can concentrate on presenting a tale of young
love with delicacy and charm. Pilar and Manuel meet one night in
the Casa de Campo area of Madrid. They greet each other reserv-
edly at first, but soon adopt the more colloquial forms of address,
"Pili" and "Manolo," which mark the recovery of their usual intimacy. Manuel becomes impatient because Pilar's mother will not
allow her to stay out late with him. The couple have a tiff, acting

out the archetypal roles of demanding male and offended female, but they cannot fall out for long and soon forgive each other. The "Ballad" closes with a highly charged scene in which the vulnerable Pilar just manages to resist Manuel's advances as they stand in the shadows, looking at the reflection of the moon in the black waters of the Manzanares.

The dramatic intensity of this story, with its mute suggestion of repressed and fragile sexuality, derives from carefully implemented rhetorical and structural devices. The lovers' private quarrel is projected against a dual background of popular scenes in the bars and streets of Madrid and features of natural scenery, so that contrasts of perspective and tone enrich the narrative.[3] The recurrent passages of natural description provide a wealth of sensual detail which anticipates Pilar and Manuel's sexual drama: the sky is dark "like phosphorus," bats screech in the cold air, and a dog barks at the moon. Such prose is an assault on the reader's senses and sensibility, and it makes "Ballad of the River Manzanares" a masterpiece of suggestion.

"La piel del verano" ("The Summer's Skin") is an adequate study of aboulia in a young man. The plot progresses with a fearful sense of inevitability as Rafael succumbs to the wily persuasion of a companion whom he does not really like. His impotence to act according to the futile dictates of his conscience is pointed up at the structural level by alternating passages of narrative and interior monologue culminating in his shameless admission that it makes no difference whom he has as a friend. With "Waiting for Autumn" and "Camino del limbo" ("Heading Nowhere"), this story shows Aldecoa's concern for the problems of disoriented youth.

"Courtyard of Arms" and "Las piedras del páramo" ("Stones of the Wilderness") both take the Spanish Civil War as their point of reference. The first story has a strong autobiographical element. The setting, in a northern province controlled by the Nationalists, is the city of Vitoria, and the mischievous schoolboy, Gamarra, is most probably a likeness of the author at twelve or thirteen years of age. But more important than this self-centered retrospection is Aldecoa's attempt to show children's reactions to the war. Occupation, the billeting of German and Italian troops, and the death and imprisonment of soldiers and political prisoners are facts which register in the boys' minds as part of a romantic adventure or game. The story opens and closes with a list of instructions for a war game, and the boys spend their recess time playing at soldiers. They look on a real soldier, a German on patrol in their school yard, as a source of amusement, and mimic his broken Castilian speech. Yet war is an immediate reality. Two men whose sons attend the school die: one, a Nationalist officer, is killed by a stray bullet, and the other, a Republican who has been taken prisoner, dies in unexplained circumstances. In a supremely ironic conclusion, their bereaved sons are shown taking part in a game of war on opposite sides, and the sound of artillery from the front can be heard in the school yard, impinging on the world of imagination.

"Stones in the Wilderness" has greater dramatic appeal than "Courtyard of Arms" and a poetic richness not found in that story. The narrative conveys an old man's perplexity and distress when the first local shots of the Civil War rudely awaken him from the routine of a passive existence. Immersed in the world of nature and indifferent to family and society, he is waiting calmly for the day when he will receive the last sacrament and die in peace. But news that the village priest has suddenly been captured fills him with indignation at the threat of abandonment and the frustration of his most cherished illusion. The story's poetic quality rests on the extraordinary cultivation of sensuous detail. Aldecoa captures vividly the perceptions of an old man, immobile, half blind, and introspective. His mind wanders from the present to the past, and from the factual world to a realm of dreams and obsessions. The world around him is one undifferentiated mass of sound in which "movement, color, size and speech" (I, 399) fuse by synaesthesia. He hears no more than echoes of reality, and sees only a murky film before him. At the end of the story his anger is expressed powerfully in apocalyptic images of deafening thunderbolts and roaring waves, appropriate to his religious sensibility. "Stones in the Wilderness" is further indication of Aldecoa's grasp of refined or heightened psychological experience.

Some aspects of narrative and structural technique in *The Picador's Mount* deserve comment. Different ways of mediating information are chosen according to a story's particular nature and purpose. For example, the choice of viewpoint in "Stones in the Wilderness" is crucial to the story's effect, since it brings out the consequences of war with added immediacy by identifying a specific human case. Similarly, narrative presentation conditions subject matter and mood in "Sister Candelas." The reader encounters elements of mystery and ambiguity in the abrupt introduction which match the eerie experience of spiritualism described in subsequent pages. One such device, anonymity of character, is used in a number of other stories: to convey a sense of universality in "The Leave Taking," and to emphasize the stifling of personality in "No Man's Land." As is usual in Aldecoa's narratives, the relation between suggestion and declaration is a matter of fine judgment.

As regards structural features, certain critics have discerned expressive figures of correspondence and opposition in such stories as "Ballad of the River Manzanares" and "The Leave Taking." Jorge Urrutia has analyzed the latter as a system of formal relations designed to figure forth the theme of human solidarity and communication.[4] In overall construction, story endings have a particularly important function in determining the impact of a narrative. The conclusions of "The Burning Sword" and "Two Hearts and One Shadow" reveal dramatic details about the characters' private lives. "Sister Candelas" closes on a note of incongruity and irony. And the apparently neutral comment which rounds off "The Picador's Mount" is aimed at provoking the reader's thoughtful condemnation of man's inhumanity to man.

Objects and natural phenomena are often endowed with symbolic significance in these stories. A sugar bowl left in the middle of a table represents the sisters' abandoned state in "Two Hearts and One Shadow." A film magazine which a fussy woman traveler uses as a fan in "The Leave Taking" symbolizes her superficiality and pettiness. At one moment in "The Burning Sword," the widowed mayor tries to grasp a ray of light which had been caught momentarily by a precious stone worn on the finger where his wedding band used to be. This unconscious gesture lays bare his nostalgia and emotional susceptibility. Imagery is thus a constant feature of Aldecoa's art.

CHAPTER 9

Subsequent Collections

I Pájaros y espantapájaros

Pájaros y espantapájaros (*Birds and Scarecrows*) consists of eleven stories. In "La chica de la Glorieta" ("The Girl at the Crossroads") the theme is prostitution. The story is set in a central district of Madrid at around two o'clock one summer's morning, when a few bored and weary people are still to be seen in this part of "the paralyzed city." Angelita, the "whore of flaccid heart" announced in a motto taken from Henry Miller's *Tropic of Cancer,* appears talking to a young waiter in a cafeteria and then to an old woman who sells cigarettes and matches. On the point of going home, she is picked up by some men in a Seat 600. The story concludes in oracular fashion as the cigarette vendor thinks how lucky Angelita has been, and utters a deep, provocative sigh. This ambiguous ending exemplifies Aldecoa's detachment from the scenes of human behavior depicted here. His attitude is neither maudlin, censorious, or controversial. As narrator he makes no intrusive remarks about Angelita whose character is tellingly exteriorized in what she says and does. The onus of moral evaluation is passed on to the reader as an optional element in his aesthetic response to the story.

"Al margen" ("On the Fringe") and "Camino del limbo" ("Heading Nowhere") are united by the common themes of passivity and boredom. The first story features three colorless people whose life of exquisite tedium revolves around lunchtime aperitifs and late-night parties. Theirs is the superficial and senseless existence of the American tourists in *Part of a Story.* Aldecoa chooses a technique of presentation which suggests exactly this quality of shallowness and unfulfilled potential. As Erna Brandenberger has pointed out, he "outlines several possible conflicts, several situations which are pregnant with consequences. The tension of the

120

story lies in the fact that he does not develop any of them."[1] "Heading Nowhere" shows the effect of a stifling provincial environment on a diffident youth, Miguel, who, with the departure of his best friend to the university, is condemned to a life of stultifying routine in a backwater city. Not only is Miguel the victim of his own indecision, he is also frustratingly aware of his inability to break out of the vicious circle in which he is enclosed. On a general level, Miguel is one of a lost generation whose situation Aldecoa had planned to analyze in *Chrysalis Years*.

The bourgeoisie comes under uncompromising attack in three stories: "El diablo en el cuerpo" ("The Devil inside Him"), "Los bisoñés de don Ramón" ("Mr. Raymond's Toupees"), and "Para los restos" ("For the Remains"). Not only is this class despised for holding a decadent moral code, but the most harmless aspects of its behavior are ridiculed and caricatured. Hypocrisy, pretense, bigotry, and selfishness are some of the qualities supposed to typify the bourgeois spirit. Female characters appear in a particularly offensive light. Doña Trini, the hysterical and infantile wife of don Eladio in the first tale, is crudely dismissed as a fat cow by one of her husband's acquaintances, and in so many words by the narrator. Doña Josefina, Mr. Raymond's mother, is pompous, self-righteous, and sycophantic, as her behavior toward her son's boss illustrates. And doña Engracia, in "For the Remains," is a tyrannical, venomous gossip whose perversity is epitomized in the relish with which she shows her friends a flask containing one dozen stones extracted, most improbably, from the body of her dead brother.

In his depiction of don Eladio, a retired army officer who owns and manages a fashion shop, Aldecoa takes the opportunity to mimic certain stock attitudes of those who, as pillars of the community, uphold the professional and moral values of the status quo. Don Eladio believes in hierarchy and authority, and in the virtues of prudent saving and investment. Preoccupied with respectability and decency, he goes insane after winning first prize in the national lottery three times running. Aldecoa's gratuitous destruction of a fictional puppet indicates the extent of his vengeful assault on bourgeois values. The narrative temper of these stories contrasts with the restraint employed in those dealing with the experience of the proletariat. There is no attempt at concealing the presence of an ebullient narrator, who makes ironic remarks and vicious gibes about the representatives of a much maligned class.

"El figón de la **Damiana**" ("Old Damiana's Kitchen") depicts an infraworld of criminals and drunkards, with liberal recourse to the distorted and grotesque trappings of tremendism. In the story a beggar has been stabbed to death at Damiana's during a card game. Two old reprobate soldiers, Antón and "El Ventura" ("Lucky"), stumble drunkenly on the corpse and are held in custody until the real culprit is identified and shot while resisting arrest. The crime becomes part of the neighborhood's collective mythology, and the excitement it produces soon dies away. Not so Antón and "Lucky's" fondness of alcohol, for one night they get into Damiana's stock of liquor and string up her one-eyed cat in a macabre scene worthy of Cela or Buñuel. Aldecoa presents the tale with perverse satisfaction and an obvious delight in the flexibility and richness of colloquial language. The "whodunit" form is not fully exploited, as the treatment of plot yields pride of place to a recreation of drunkenness, vulgarity, and violence.

"Un artista llamado Faisán" ("An Artist Called Pheasant") is a subtle and compassionate character study of a long-suffering but dignified vagabond. "Pheasant" earns an insecure living at the fairs in the Ebro area by making floral designs, composing poetry, singing operatic excerpts, or simply by mending shoes. One night he is beaten up by Mencía and Lavoz, two jealous rivals whom he had accused of professional double-dealing. During the police inquiry he magnanimously saves them from certain imprisonment by denying their guilt, even though he must now enter the hospital for treatment of a tubercular condition aggravated by the assault. "Pheasant" is characteristically brave and good-humored there, but dies one evening after a conciliatory visit from Mencía and Lavoz. On the day of the funeral the two guilty companions fail to reach the cemetery, succumbing instead to the temptation of a glass of beer and plate of tripe in a nearby village. They pay their final, drunken respects to "Pheasant" by singing a couple of ballads when they pass the cemetery on their way home.

The reticence with which Aldecoa treats the question of morality does not lessen the force of his condemnation of egoism and indifference. He clearly supports the cause of the underdog and social victim, and promotes the virtues of resignation and generosity, tacitly censuring Mencía and Lavoz for their thoughtlessness. But he is also tolerant of human imperfections, appreciating that "Pheasant's" eccentricities may sometimes not command admiration but scorn, and that Mencía and Lavoz's delinquency is not wholly malicious, being in part the result of ignorance. Aldecoa contemplates humanity with concern, pathos, and occasional black humor as a defense against sentimentality. Colloquial and ironic expressions vary the tone in a story remarkable for its formal balance and technical economy.

"Pájaros y espantapájaros" ("Birds and Scarecrows") was originally published under the straightforward title of "Las cuatro baladas extrañas" ("The Four Strange Ballads"). It is a bizarre tale about four peddlers from different corners of Spain who meet quite by chance at a roadside inn, share a frugal meal, and tell of their respective lives. Late in the afternoon they all fall asleep, each man having a fabulous dream which the narrator presents in the form of a ballad. The first ballad concerns a child's search for the unique "blue bat," reputed to bring good luck to him who finds it; the second tells of an eerie moonlight romance, and the third, of a fantastic journey inside an emerald; the fourth ballad is about a man who talks to his fingers, one of which is broken and actually "in receipt of a pension" (I, 342). When they wake up, the four peddlers go their separate ways, never to meet again.

A persuasive narrator introduces the reader into the independent world of fantasy, and throughout invokes a spurious authority — a Cervantine scribe or copyist — to explain the origin of the four ballads. Aldecoa cultivates absurdity for its own sake, disregarding any extraliterary factors — moral or social — which might violate the hermetic character of his extravaganza. The story is full of conceits:

El juglar gallego se quedó dormido, abrazándose la cabeza, temeroso de que se la robasen; el juglar baztanés se echó hacia atrás, la gorra sobre los ojos, la boca entreabierta, la nariz como una rara turbina absorbiendo el aire. (337)

The minstrel [peddler] from Galicia dropped off to sleep, his arms wrapped around his head for fear someone might steal it; the one from Baztán leaned back, with his cap over his eyes, his mouth wide open, his nose like a weird sort of turbine taking in the air.

Abrió el mago la carraca de su navaja para cortar una cuerdecilla pendona que le sobraba del costal y llegó la Semana Santa. (342)

The magician opened his old clasp knife to cut a loose thread off the sack he was carrying, and Holy Week arrived.

Religious vocabulary, including the words "sacramental," "sacer-
dotal," and "liturgical," establishes a nonsensical analogy in keeping with the overall atmosphere of carefully fabricated absurdity.

II Arqueología

Imagination, humor, and sensitivity to emotion are qualities
which Aldecoa continues to practice in the stories included in
Arqueología (*Archaeology*). His imagination comes into play in
three stories which Alicia Bleiberg has classified under the heading
"Vidas extrañas" ("Strange Lives") because of the eccentric
characters and life-style they present. They are "El asesino" ("The
Assassin"), "El caballero de la anécdota" ("The Gentleman with a
Story about Him"), and "El libelista Benito" ("Benito the Libelist"). The first story in the volume, "La vuelta al mundo" ("The
Trip around the World"), may be considered along with them. In
retirement, Eusebio kills time by playing "Ludo" with his accom-
modating wife, Clara, and dreaming of imposing deeds and sea
voyages from the safety of his armchair. Another imaginative conception is Anthony, the half-English, half-Spanish protagonist of
"The Assassin." Anthony owns a barber's shop in the heart of
flamenco Andalucía, and has a name in the feminine for each of
the razors he uses on his customers. He once killed an unfaithful
girl friend with one, fatally underestimating its sharpness.

The possibilities of humor in absurd or improbable situations are
brilliantly realized in "Benito the Libelist," a lively caricature of
an eccentric composer of defamatory and satirical verse, dedica-
tions, and miscellaneous trivia. Aldecoa fashions this piece of levity
with a Cervantine brand of irony founded on antithesis. First, there
is a disparity between Benito's lofty ideals — his passionate dedication to the cause of freedom — and his ineffectuality. When he discovers that an important article in the day's newspaper has been
censured, he rushes to a local bar where his "co-revolutionaries"
usually gather, to decide on measures to defend "the temple of
Liberty" (I, 323). Having improvised a couple of innocuous
insults, he loses patience with the other members of the group who
cannot agree on a united plan of action, turns to the bottle for consolation, and eventually returns home singing, aptly, the *Marseil-
laise*. Then, there is a contrast between Benito and Matilde, his no-
nonsense wife. Matilde represents all that is down-to-earth, practical, and prosaic: she has "a fat face like a Swiss cow's udder"

(321) and enjoys eating, gossiping, and looking after the pet canaries. Benito is no match for her when he comes home drunk, for she
disposes of him with a free assortment of blows and insults.
"Benito the Libelist" is contrived with the same ingenious flare as
"The Folk from Andin Lane."

In two autobiographical tales, "Aldecoa se burla" ("Aldecoa
Has a Laugh") and "Maese Zaragosí y Aldecoa su huésped"
("Master Zaragosi and Aldecoa his Lodger"), humor is again prom-
ent, partly at the expense of a character singled out for ridicule. In
the second story it is Master Zaragosi who is subjected to ungra-
cious treatment because he has a weak bladder. But the comic elements rest mainly on the author's willful narcissism, whether he
depicts himself as an insolent child of fourteen getting the better of
a schoolmaster or as a penniless and irresponsible student who
never fails to talk himself out of trouble, especially when inconti-
nence impedes his landlord-opponent from developing fully, let
alone winning, an argument. Aldecoa supports this autobiographical indulgence by quoting authorities as respectable as Erasmus of
Rotterdam and Simone de Beauvoir on the need of self-esteem.

That quality of sensibility which in earlier volumes distinguished
stories like "He Only Wanted to Rest in Peace" and "The Heart
and Other Bitter Fruits" is to be found here in "La nostalgia de
Lorenza Ríos" ("Lorenza Ríos' Homesickness") and "Crónica de
los novios del ferial" ("Chronicle of the Fairground Lovers").
Lorenza Ríos, a Mexican, comes to Spain with her common-law
husband and two daughters, and lives a melancholy life. She is
gradually left alone: her no-good husband drowns, her two girls
marry and leave home, her son in Mexico has written only twice in
so many years. She dies, "shedding her last tears" in a cemetery
overlooking the Cantabrian sea. *Iteratio* in passages of narrative,
and asyndeton in descriptive sections are figures of speech which
restrain tempo and assist in establishing a uniform mood of pensive
sadness.

The world of circus and fairground entertainment, celebrated
previously in twentieth-century Spanish art by Baroja and Picasso,
is the setting of "Chronicle of the Fairground Lovers." Enrique
and Margarita work in the Circus Theatre, dancing under the
incongruous stage name of "The Anthony Sisters." They are not
long married; he is jealous and possessive, she loving but coquet-
tish. Enrique claims that Margarita has given the glad eye to a man
in the front row of the audience, and slaps her face as soon as their

performance is over. The story is built around this incident and uncovers the meaningful fragment in the prosaic course of life. It is constructed with purpose and care. Narrative attention shifts from the broad scene of the fairground to the crude theater, and comes to rest on the young couple and their private drama. There is a fitting change of tone when the festive atmosphere becomes restrained and intimate. This and the previous story prove once more Aldecoa's gift for capturing and conveying varying degrees of human emotion.

III   Critical Appraisal

Although "Birds and Scarecrows," "Benito the Libelist," and "Chronicle of the Fairground Lovers" represent Aldecoa at his best, the overall effect of *Birds and Scarecrows* and *Archaeology* is disappointing. In a review of the first, one critic stated: "This book adds nothing to the body of Aldecoa's work, apart from a few good stories which suffocate in the general context of the volume."[2] The ten stories in *Archaeology* unfortunately do little to remedy this impression.

CHAPTER 10

The Last Stories

I   Los pájaros de Baden Baden

L os pájaros de Baden Baden (*The Birds of Baden Baden*) comprises four mature compositions whose formal properties immediately pose the teasing problem of whether they should be classified as "short novels" or simply as "long stories." José Ramón Marra López chooses the first alternative with vague reservations;[1] Erna Brandenberger considers one of the compositions an example of what she somewhat flexibly and contentiously calls "a story with the structure of a short novel or a similar structure."[2] Rather than wrestle with such unamenable distinctions, it is prudent to stick within the bounds of empirical observation and indicate those features which unite and distinguish the four stories. They vary in length between approximately four and a half and eleven thousand words, and cover periods of time ranging from a few days to several months. They exhibit a diversity of plot and multiplicity of characters not permitted in the short story form. And they resemble the novel in that they allow for psychological development, and incorporate sustained patterns of imagery of the kind found in *Blood and Lightning*.

"Un buitre ha hecho su nido en el café" ("A Buzzard Has Made its Nest in the Café") is a narrative in eight sections which traces the fortunes of Raimundo and his mistress, Encarna, over a period of some four days or more. Each evening Raimundo takes Encarna to a dingy cafeteria, leaving her alone and exposed to the leers and advances of other men while he plays cards in the gameroom. At first he loses heavily and cannot keep his promise of buying her an expensive present. That Saturday night he wins handsomely, but discovers that in his absence, Encarna has run off with a rich, elderly gentleman who had taken to sitting with her. In accordance

127

with popular belief, Raimundo ends up lucky at cards but unlucky in love.

The plot of this story is discontinuous. Each section describes events in the café at a particular point in time, with no account of what happens between periods or from one evening to the next. Such a method of presentation makes it difficult to determine the actual duration of the action. However, the structural pattern is not intended as a reflection of naturalistic time. Rather, it corresponds to the movements of a game of chess, an analogy central to the whole story. First, characters are referred to in symbolic terms: Raimundo is a knight and Encarna, a queen; Damián the cigarette vendor, who is called upon to act as a go-between by a customer angling for Encarna's company, is termed a "peón de enlace" — literally, a "linking pawn" — and so on. Second, the black and white tables in the café resemble a disorderly chessboard, with the characters changing places according to rules of social behavior. Third, people's movements and interaction are summarized in section headings taken from the vocabulary of chess: "Apertura" ("Opening Gambit"), "Salto de caballo" ("Knight's Move"), "Juego de alfil" ("The Bishop to Play"), etc.

The final two headings are slightly incongruous but nevertheless appropriate. Section 7, which shows the sophisticated gentleman's first overture to Encarna, echoes the story's title. Raimundo's earlier remark, that all men are like buzzards when they see a woman sitting alone, now rebounds cruelly on him as a stranger preys on Encarna. Section 8 bears the heading "Pura sangre" ("Pedigree"), a reference to the old gentleman's wealth and breeding, and an unfavorable reflection on Raimundo who had been introduced in section 2 as a "percherón," or horse of impure stock, and then in section 5 as a "palafrén" ("palfrey"). He is also the "caballo," which in Spanish means both "knight" and "horse."

The chess analogy is particularly apt in this story of gambling and fortune. It also provides an ironic gloss on the characters involved. Chess requires qualities of circumspection and forethought patently lacking in the self-centered, inconsiderate Raimundo, but which the suave gentleman possesses in abundance. Raimundo consequently appears as the victim of his own shortsightedness, the loser in a game of secrecy and calculation to which he is not equal. Although it is not Aldecoa's practice to point the finger of blame, he is clearly suggesting that Raimundo's selfishness and complacency have brought about his downfall.

It would nevertheless be unjust and simplistic to reduce the story to a moral argument, since it is made up of so many elements of style and content. Mood, for instance, is an important factor. An atmosphere of vulgarity and decay is evoked in the opening section. Windows in the cafeteria are dirty, and the light so weak that the whole scene suggests "a surreal nightmare" (II, 99). A cat, "sumido en el *haschich* de su *taedium vitae*" ("immersed in the hashish of ennui"), takes refuge on a sofa "en el que reposa el fantasma de la melancollu del tiempo pasado" ("whereon rests the ghostlike melancholy of time past," 100). Subsequently, words of malice and disrespect are exchanged among certain of the clients. Above all, there is a sense of sexual vulnerability implied in the dominant image of a buzzard preying on human flesh. The voice of a detached narrator offers no guarantee of the quality of life in this nightmarish world. "A Buzzard Has Made Its Nest in the Café" may be seen as a dense web of mental, emotional, and sensual impressions which commands a total response from the reader.

"El silbo de la lechuza" ("The Owl's Hoot") is a mischievous satire of provincial life. Aldecoa conjures up a capricious world of small-minded eccentrics sustained by gossip and petty intrigue. Two elderly sisters, Lucía and Matildita Martínez, epitomize the provincial mentality, spying on their fellow citizens with the aid of binoculars and mirrors fixed to strategic points on their balcony. They also despatch Lucía's forty-year-old son, Cayetano, to collect information concerning people like Marcelino Ayalde, the bank manager, and Juan Alegre, recently widowed. Perico Valle, the police chief, is frankly envious of their intimate knowledge of what is going on in the city.

Crime, intrigue, and romance flourish simultaneously in an array of plots and subplots. Perico and some of his associates decide to play a mean trick on Lucía and Matildita by sending a poison pen letter in which they expose Cayetano's secret relationship with a cobbler's daughter. The sisters respond by writing anonymous notes to two quite innocent gentlemen. In the meantime, their friend Doña Úrsula Villangómez plots against the bank manager, who is eventually found guilty of fraud. Cayetano and Isabelita bring their love out into the open and make plans to marry. On one of their romantic walks they overhear Juan Alegre addressing his wife's tomb and boasting that he murdered her. Cayetano makes some investigations and by Saturday night the widower has given himself up to the police. These four strands are knitted together in joyful disregard for probability, providing interest and excitement throughout the story's thirty-three pages.

The value of "The Owl's Hoot" is simply its capacity to amuse and entertain. Setting, character, and plot are treated with comic hyperbole. The first section offers a "panorámica caprichosa," or whimsical view, of the city, in a mock litany of social types and attitudes. Two of the funniest characters in the story are Matacán and Escachapobres, the barbaric policemen whose names mean literally "Killdog" and "Crush-the-poor." Humorous detail proliferates: Lucía and Matildita live in "la calle de la Libertad" ("Freedom Street"), and Doña Ursula forsakes Saint Michael's Church for Saint Peter's because gossip is more plentiful there. Even isolated words and phrases contribute to the general sense of fun. The verb "pajarear" — "to squawk" — captures the sourness inherent in one of Doña Ursula's remarks to Ayalde (II, 129). Facile but effective humor appears in the oxymoron "pulcros horteras" (113), and in the pejorative reference to "sólidos burgueses en compañía de sus elefantas" ("solid bourgeois citizens with their lady elephants," 115). The last laugh is reserved for the narrator who has a privileged, bird's-eye view of this quaint and frivolous world.

This hilarious spirit is carried over into the third story of the volume, "Ave de Paraíso" ("Bird of Paradise"), which is defined in the following preface: "Los personajes de esta historia nada tienen que ver con personajes de la vida real. Pertenecen a un mundo alegre y siniestro, híbrido de opereta y guiñol. Lo que aquí se cuenta es solamente un disparate" ("The characters in this story bear no relation to any person in real life. They belong to a ludicrous and sinister world which combines elements from the soap opera and puppet show. The story told here is just a piece of nonsense," II, 330). Although this peculiar world of beatniks, Latin lovers, and compliant female tourists has its roots in Ibiza, a Mediterranean island and center of tourism well known to Aldecoa and his family, it is most fully appreciated as the product of literary fantasy. The stylized setting, absurd and stereotyped characters, capricious motivation of plot, and self-conscious narrative style leave no doubt as to the accuracy of the author's prefatory remarks.

"Bird of Paradise" begins with some descriptive scenes of a coastal resort which highlight its unusual and indecorous features. Metaphors and conceits underline the narrative's mannered quality; comic antithesis and incongruence of style are basic to its technique. At the end of each paragraph a mysterious character, Barón

Samedi, is evoked in awe and expectation. In section 2, the focus shifts to a bar haunted by beatniks, bohemians, and decadents. It is a center of worship for these "faithful parishioners" who come to indulge in "liturgical" experiences. The atmosphere in the bar is heavy with the smoke of marijuana and the sound of jazz. Some characters are identified by name; the bartender is called "El Gran Barbudo" ("The Great Bearded One"); one of the beatniks is called Iphigeneia, and the rest, "Captain Kid's extras" (II, 332). This practice of ironically drawing names from mythology and cheap comic literature extends throughout the story.

Barón Samedi appears in person in section 3, being introduced as "Lord of the Graveyards and Chief of the Legion of the Dead" (333). He is a lascivious, haughty, and sinister man who devotes himself to the pursuit of pleasure. His name originates in Voodoo ritual, and is connected with popular superstition about the practice of magic and witchcraft on Saturdays. Samedi has a rival called "The King" or "Caesar," whose achievements as a playboy have earned him fame and respect all over the island. The King has an entourage of three parasitical men known as the Marquis of the North, the Marquis of the South, and the Viscount of the Riviera, and a bad tempered Alsatian bitch called Isabel. Currently disenchanted with life, he dreams of escaping to a distant paradise. The story is entitled "Bird of Paradise" after him. Section 5 gives an illustration of the King's power over women, and shows how Samedi is always second best in matters of love. The King once stole a Danish girl from Samedi; although she is still infatuated with him, he now treats her with cold disdain. Samedi meets her and tries to win her back, but she inflicts a symbolic defeat on him by rejecting his overtures.

An exchange of words between Samedi and the King at the end of section 6 portends a major articulation in the narrative. The King overhears Samedi announcing the arrival of a German girl friend called Tusa, and promptly declares his intention of taking her from him. He does so in the following section, and the many consequences of his treachery are dealt with in the remainder of the story. Samedi calls on everybody to ostracize the King for not playing fair. The "boycott" lasts until the arrival of spring, when the King resolves to leave the island. But first he throws a magnificent farewell party attended by Samedi, his friends, and colorful types like Baroness Cocktail and other *aficionados* of the *dolce vita*. After the party the King is fighting drunk and causes a rumpus near the harbor which lands him in jail. He remains there for some days, spoiled by the attentions of numerous adoring female visitors. Once free, he loses no time in gathering his belongings and setting sail for Southern Paradise.

The increase in tempo from section 7 onward is accompanied by an unflagging mood of mock gravity. Clichés are an effective source of humor. Infuriated by "the inconstant Tusa's" defection, Samedi instigates nothing less than "a conspiracy" against the King, and invokes a noble code of chivalry. In his drunken rage, the King challenges three local thugs, The Killer Brothers, to fight him, and the contest is recounted as a battle between a royal legion and an army comprising light cavalry and assault troops. This spirit of parody is reflected in the subtitle of section 15, "El rey se va, viva el rey" ("The King is Leaving, God Save the King"). The story closes with a rhythmic chant from the sea, in honor of the King's departure. It is a conclusion which reinforces the impression of a fabulous fairy tale.

Both Gaspar Gómez de la Serna and Manuel García Viñó regard "Bird of Paradise" as a landmark in Aldecoa's prose. The first critic noted the growing frequency and skill with which Aldecoa cultivated the *jácara,* or "festive ballad," in the absurd tradition of the *esperpento.*[3] García Viñó sees "Bird of Paradise" as a pioneering work heralding unprecedented developments in the realm of fiction.[4] Although the story has obvious forerunners in Aldecoa's earlier production, namely, in "Biography of a Figurehead," "The Assaults in Lime Village," and "The Folk from Andin Lane," its internal consistency and self-sufficiency make it an incomparable piece of invention.

"The Birds of Baden Baden" exemplifies Aldecoa's skill in the more conventional field of social and psychological realism. Set in Madrid during the long summer recess, the story describes the disorientation and frustrations of a thirty-four year old single woman, Elisa, who remains in the city in order to finish writing a psychology textbook. Elisa makes no progress with this project because of the constant distractions of her relations with three men. She is pursued relentlessly by two individuals, Ricardo and Pedro, who are taking advantage of temporary freedom while their families are away on holidays. But it is a young photographer and artist called Pablo who interests her most and with whom she falls in love. Unfortunately Pablo fails to reciprocate her feelings, and she is overcome with bitter disappointment as summer draws to a close.

The economical range of contrasting characters, and the depth in which Aldecoa probes the inward turns of their minds are adequate compensation for the unoriginal plot. Elisa is a unique creation in Aldecoa's novels and stories. She is a complex woman whose individuality resides in the tensions between her powerful intellect and unstable emotions. Her sharp perceptions and irrepressible tendency to introspection reflect her professional training as a psychologist. An intellectual, she has no difficulty in coping with Ricardo's transparent hypocrisies and predictable maneuvers, and finds Pedro's superior intelligence a challenge and attraction. Emotionally, however, she cannot fend for herself. She hankers after the artificial security of an irrecoverable childhood, and is unable to look upon Pedro as anything other than a protective father figure. She falls for Pablo because he is young, dynamic, spontaneous, and sufficiently unconventional as to break down her mental and emotional defenses.

Of the three male characters, Pablo is the most individualized. His youthful irresponsibility makes him shy away from permanent relationships which he fears might curtail his freedom. Yet he is lively and good humored, an inoffensive and engaging character. Ricardo, on the other hand, is nothing more than a stereotype. He represents the adulterous middle-class male who will feign and stoop to anything in order to win the sympathy and favors of one of his wife's friends. Pedro stands somewhere in between the type and the individual. The impression that he is little more than an abstraction stems in part from the fact that he makes only three brief appearances in the narrative. He is a counterpart to Elisa in that his authoritative manner and tendency to intellectualize are obstacles to the necessary expression of his emotions. His potential is nevertheless left unfulfilled in the story. The illuminating contrast between these three characters is brought out by the constant shifting of the narrative from one to another.

Imagery is an essential vehicle for the conveyance of mood and meaning in "The Birds of Baden Baden." The story opens with a symbolic picture of an area in Madrid. Sitting on a terrace overlooking a busy street, Elisa imagines herself on a quayside gazing out to sea. A whole chain of equivalences derives from this simile. Elisa makes out the silhouettes of distant parks and buildings to be jetties, the noise of trains and cars evokes the mechanical bustle of harbors, while the River Manzanares becomes a paralyzed and silvery sea monster. This interiorized landscape introduces the reader inside Elisa's distracted mind, since it functions as an expression of her nostalgia for childhood, when she would spend her summer holiday by the sea. One of the images, which depicts a shoal of fish devouring one another in bloody brutality, foreshadows the cruelty and suffering she is to undergo. Her apathy and lack of purpose are subsequently portrayed in the image of a body floating motionless on the sea. The idea of physical danger is contained in a second group of images which refer to the hunting, trapping, wounding, and killing of animals. In one such instance, Pedro stalks Elisa and conceives of her as a sacrificial victim. Finally, there is the figure of Don Quixote which catches Elisa's attention while Ricardo is speaking to her on the telephone. The model symbolizes her emotional and sexual instability. She notices how the sword is limp and bent, and how the shield is useless protection against some undefined danger. She twists the sword completely in a gesture of frustration and revenge.

II   *Separate Items*

In the four years prior to his death, Aldecoa wrote as many new stories, of which two are of limited interest. "La noche de los grandes peces" ("The Night of the Big Fishes") and "Party" date from 1965. The first is a rather forced reconstruction of an actual event from Aldecoa's life. While staying on the island of Ibiza in 1961, he had gone on a fishing trip with two friends.[5] The story tries to capture the enthusiasm and excitement of that adventure, but goes no further than revelling in self-glory. The narrative of "Party" presents a critique of bourgeois mores by recreating the thoughts and obsessions of a moody husband who is waiting for his forty-year-old wife to return from a social event. The anonymous couple's marriage is seen to rest on foundations of suspicion, frustration, and disrespect. In a bathetic anticlimax to the man's expectations, his wife returns home and they exchange a few banal comments which show the irremediable emptiness and artificiality of their relationship.

Aldecoa's next creation was "Amadís" (1968), a tale which Janet Díaz has analyzed in profitable detail. According to this critic, Aldecoa pretended in this story to expose "certain absurdities of contemporary upper class society," and to denounce "the moral decadence and general degradation in our time of human values."[6] He accomplished his aim by adopting the method of parodic inversion of the conventions of chivalric literature. The title, "Amadís," is taken from an early sixteenth-century chivalric novel, *Amadís de Gaula;* but the psychology, atmosphere, events, and ideals of that uplifting model are systematically debased. In this way Aldecoa satirizes modern society, the self-interest and materialism of which are exemplified in the figure of his chevalier *manqué,* Amadís. The story illustrates both the continuity of spirit and intention, and the process of technical sophistication in Aldecoa's work since he wrote "The Market" in the early fifties.

"A Heart Humble and Tired" is chronologically the last of Aldecoa's compositions. As already noted in our biographical section, there is an eerie coincidence between this story about a young man, Toni, who is recovering from a heart attack, and Aldecoa's state of health. "A Heart Humble and Tired" conveys a powerful sense of mystery and fright as disturbing as that in a story by Edgar Allan Poe. In the final section a terrified Toni overhears a stranger pleading with his father to certify the death of his son. Aldecoa's style reaches an appropriate level of refinement in "A Heart Humble and Tired." The opening paragraphs exhibit his resourceful use of rhetorical devices including simile, metaphor, chiasmus, and antithesis.

III *Final Stories: a Conclusion*

After the comparative mediocrity of *Archaeology* and *Birds and Scarecrows, The Birds of Baden Baden* and other pieces came as a timely reaffirmation of Aldecoa's talent as a *cuentista.* They are a lasting reminder of his powers of observation and invention, control of composition and expression, and his sensitivity to significant detail in the rendering of character, background, and atmosphere.

CHAPTER 11

Travel Literature and an Epic Documentary

I *Travel Literature: Articles and* Cuaderno de godo

BETWEEN 1953 and 1962 Aldecoa published occasional accounts of his experience as a seasoned traveler. This part of his creative output comprises two books of moderate length, and a number of articles and reports for various publications. Though Aldecoa traveled abroad extensively after 1959, he confined himself to studies of the Spanish panorama. His first report, "Alava, provincia en cuarto menguante" ("Alava, a Province in its Last Quarter"), appeared in January 1953 and was later incorporated in a guide book to the Basque country. A short piece on the Levantine interior, "Viaje a Filabres" ("A Trip to Filabres"), followed in 1954. A year later, on his return from the *jornadas literarias* to Alta Extremadura, Aldecoa wrote "An Urgent Return Journey." To Gaspar Gómez de la Serna, himself an author of works in the travel genre, the first of these short pieces seemed a lighthearted and simple exercise whereas the second demonstrated greater commitment to social factors, being "a painful immersion of the soul in a hopeless corner of tragic Spain with all its desolation, backwardness, and poverty." The same critic regarded "Urgent Return Journey" as marking the point in Aldecoa's development as a writer of travel literature at which he began to subordinate social concerns to aesthetic values, "making of his work a pure literary creation rather than a poignant documentary."[1] In that essay memory functioned as a poetic agent, infusing the narrative with exquisite melancholy and nostalgia.

The newspaper articles which Aldecoa wrote during his first visit to the Canary Islands in 1957 were refashioned into a more extensive and unified work, *Cuaderno de godo* (*A Goth's Notebook*).

136

Dedicated to the *tinerfeños* José Arocena and Domingo Pérez Minik, and illustrated by Chumy Chúmez, this insubstantial booklet derives its title from the use of the word "godo" in Canary speech to distinguish peninsular Spaniards from the native *canarios*. In chapter 1 Aldecoa respectfully acknowledges the obligations incumbent on an outsider. The "godo" must respect the norms of those communities he visits; he must not adopt a superior or condescending attitude, nor indulge in academic analyses of customs not his own: "He must take the islands as they come, that is, naturally."[2] The author modestly describes *A Goth's Notebook* as "just a few superficial notes from an easygoing trip around the islands..." (14). The book is consequently rich in aesthetic perceptions, but devoid of tendentious opinions. It is nearer to poetry than documentary: generally the technique is impressionistic, the mood nostalgic, the language connotative.

Aldecoa soon discovers the poverty of conventional attitudes to the Canaries, as exemplified in the teaching of geography at school. But he observes perceptively the rich variety of natural and cultural phenomena there, and is able to augment and improve on commonplace views. Ten of the thirteen chapters deal in turn with the seven major islands and the secondary groups. The narrator comments on the linguistic peculiarities of Puerto de la Luz, in Gran Canaria, where the wily natives converse and barter with gullible foreigners in *pichinglis,* employing Spanish pronunciation and English vocabulary in an awkward but colorful combination. La Palma provokes reflections on mythology and history. The archangel Saint Michael is supposed to protect the island from natural disasters such as volcanic eruptions and storms, and from sundry human menaces, of which piracy was the most serious in the sixteenth century. Tenerife exercises a particular fascination, with its twin cities, Santa Cruz and La Laguna, its varied climate, and imposing geography; words cannot express the beauty of Tenerife.

Literary reminiscences of, for example, Cervantes, Shakespeare, and Hemingway, figure in some chapters. Folklore and social tradition are discussed in others. A wedding or the launching of a boat are outstanding events in the community life of Corralejo on Fuerteventura, where the usual recreations are drinking and *tertulias*. La Graciosa, the real counterpart of the island setting in *Part of a Story,* receives close attention in chapter 12. A small cemetery of just two graves on the desolate beach at La Graciosa moves the narrator to think about death, in a preview of the themes and setting of *Part of a Story.*

A Goth's Notebook ends with a speculative chapter on the magical lost island of San Borondón: "A ghost or reflected image, a sigh from Atlantis or a medieval enchantment, an ancient dream or modern illusion, San Borondón is drifting freely" (54). Information gathered from certain maps and naval documents complements the alluring hypotheses of myth in an artistic synthesis. As the author freely admitted, the notebook is loosely constructed and indulgent, but its charm and simplicity may nevertheless be enjoyed in the same unpretentious spirit in which the work was composed.

II   *Travel Literature:* El país vasco

It is fitting that Aldecoa should have contributed the volume about his native Basque country for the Guías de España (Guides to Spain) series. But there were certain generic specifications with which the author was required to comply, for commercial and political reasons. Sponsored by the Spanish government, this collection caters to an international tourist readership at best *amateur,* at worst philistine, and is designed to promote, persuade, and sell. *El país vasco* (*The Basque Country*) is accordingly a catalog of necessarily selected information presented in a schematic form and written in attractive, accessible prose.

The book comprises a general introduction, three sections on the individual provinces: Alava, Guipuzcoa, and Vizcaya, and a conclusion devoted to the customs and lore of the area. Aldecoa begins by offering his services to the tourist-reader and establishing .his point of view: "When I speak about this region I do not offer a judgment or opinion, but an emotion. An emotion made up of shadows familiar to me, rain falling with a melody I have always remembered, mountains I have seen silhouetted in the sun, covered in mist, capped with snow...."[3] He defines his approach again in the concluding section: "The traveler's heart is hunting emotions with a nostalgic future" (57). This lyrical aesthetic is accompanied by a spirit of freewheeling adventure and a preference for the personally chosen, as opposed to the established itinerary.

Though inspired by a similar outlook, *The Basque Country* is longer, more coherent, and less contemplative than *A Goth's Notebook*. It opens with a conventional summary of the principal divisions in Basque history, including a list of local celebrities in the fields of art, literature, and politics. There follows an account of the region's physical geography: "fishing nets, ferns and chimneys symbolize the landscape of Biscay and Guipuzcoa" (10). The narrator succeeds in painting an unexpectedly attractive picture of the industrial capital, Bilbao, before pondering on the rugged beauty and economic importance of the extensive Basque coastline.

The history of Alava may be appreciated through a survey of its ancient dolmens, Roman roads, and Romanesque and Gothic churches, Aldecoa shows great interest in church architecture, mentioning the names of planners, builders, and masons, and the style and age of the various parts, in a factual manner which excludes sentimental reverie. This province offers such recreational pursuits as cave exploration, mountaineering, and trout fishing; Rioja wine is also produced in Alava. The author's sensitivity to the effect of economic development on social relations and cultural conditions appears in the section on Guipuzcoa, which betrays his romantic nostalgia for a wholesome, primitive society. Dubious industrial progress has made Guipuzcoa the most densely populated province in Spain, but the ships still leave Pasajes de San Pedro and San Juan on their way to Great Sole, while the port of Zarauz, important in the days of whale fishing, evokes the spirit of a heroic, pragmatic past. Meanwhile, back on *terra firma* the aesthete may view Ignacio Zuloaga's private collection of paintings by Goya and El Greco, at his house in the village of Zumaya. The third Basque province, Biscay, impresses as a monument to enterprise and materialism, "more like a huge city than a small province" (48). It is dominated by Bilbao, an industrial and commercial center with its Museum of Fine Arts containing works by Regoyos and one original Gauguin. The estuary and coastal surrounds bring to the narrator's impressionable mind the seafaring adventures of Shantí Andía and other characters created by Pío Baroja.

Aldecoa's respect for Basque culture comes to the fore in the section on popular customs. Certain musical instruments like the "chistu" and "tamboril," which are peculiar to the regions unsullied by Castilian manners, express the uniqueness of Basque culture. Many of its songs are "infused with solemn melancholy, gentle sadness, a blend of woodland murmurs, rainy days, noises from the sea" (58–59), and show nature's pervasive influence. Next the author, himself an accomplished cook, enthuses about the mouth-watering specialties of Basque cuisine, adding that certain Masonic societies uphold male privilege by reserving restaurant facilities for men only. Some sports are peculiar to the region, the most famous one being *jai-alai* or *pelota vasca;* competitions in woodcutting and cross-country running are natural in such a rural environment. Aldecoa's search for *lo castizo,* or authentic traditional detail, then takes him into the taverns where card games are played over a glass of wine called a "chiquito" in Bilbao and San Sebastián, but a "pote" in Vitoria. Proud about such a connection with his *patria chica,* the author informs us that Saint Ignatius, his namesake, is the patron saint of Biscay and Guipuzcoa. The festivities associated with this and other figures are a vital, if routine, part of popular culture: "But the program is of little importance; what really matters is the excitement spreading throughout the community, and the enthusiasm for the celebrations" (66). The *fiestas* of small country towns have the greatest charm, it is claimed. The final section closes with an informed appreciation of the Basque language, from which the author borrows the word "agur" to take his leave of the reader.

Despite the inevitable limitations implied in writing this type of work, Aldecoa succeeds in imprinting his personal stamp on *The Basque Country.* His sincere enthusiasm, extensive interests, and lyrical capacity are appropriate and engaging. But his occasionally naive costumbrism will not satisfy the progressive social critic, and the politically committed reader will search in vain for any reference to the Basque nationalist question, including the idiosyncratic position of Navarre, themes obviously precluded from a text of this sort. When compared with other contemporary Spanish novelists who have cultivated travel literature, such as Juan Goytisolo and Miguel Delibes, Aldecoa stands out as an artist whose sensibility transforms the objects of his attention through an ambivalent method which adds beauty but subtracts drama and controversy from the panorama of reality.

III   Neutral Corner

Neutral Corner (1962) is an unusual book which confounds accepted notions of genre. It totals some four and a half thousand words and combines fourteen narrative fragments on the subject of boxing, with photographs taken by Ramón Masats of gymnasia, changing rooms, and boxing rings. The juxtapositions are charged with force and suggestion: one picture of an isolated figure huddled against a radiator introduces a section of the text which presents the ruminations of an introverted boxer before a fight. Another example is an image of the moon, faintly visible through a skylight, which is printed alongside its negative, thus aptly illustrating the subject of section four, "El boxeador que perdió su sombra" ("The Boxer who Lost His Shadow").[4] Some photographs are dark and shaded, and focus close in on blows and clinches. Others offer a broad and contrasting perspective of space and color: for instance, the study of a prostrate fighter shielded by a figure whose dark suit stands out vividly against the white gowns of two attendant doctors and the expansive gray background of the canvas ring.

As regards Aldecoa's text, Erna Brandenberger ventures to define *Neutral Corner* as "a development of the conventional story form."[5] From a vantage point both physically and emotionally "neutral," a figure who is half-narrator, half-reporter records various moments of activity in and out of the ring. The units are set in a chronological framework. In the first, the reporter has taken up a position at the ringside as a fight is about to start. In the final unit he writes his account of the fight and hands it to the editor of a newspaper. But within this framework there is no coherent chronological development. The other twelve fragments refer to a number of people and situations outside the spatiotemporal scope of the reporter's assignment. Some of the units have plots in miniature, others capture a moment's experience. Each one is a self-contained tableau, sketched concisely and in detail. We see one amateur boxer working as a stevedore to finance himself, and others being talked through a training session. Throughout, Aldecoa portrays the gamut of a boxer's emotions and moods: hatred and determination, courage and cowardice, jubilation in victory and dejection in defeat. He also represents the point of view of all involved: fighter, audience, managers, reporters. He turns the tables on the audience who consider a boxing contest to be a spectacle for their entertainment: from inside the ring, a fighter is too concerned with survival to view them with anything more than indifference. Due credit is also given to managers, one of whom in section 10 secures a strategic victory over a better opponent through cunning judgment and sage counsel. This multiperspective approach in the end furnishes a composite view of the conflicting realities which make up the singular profession of boxing.

In spite of its unique appearance and generic peculiarity, *Neutral Corner* is assimilated into the main body of Aldecoa's work by virtue of the author's compassionate vision and poetic treatment of his subject. The topical facts of life in the ring are weighed against the truth about life in the ring. A special form of presentation is required and Aldecoa alternates between a realistic and an epic mode. He debunks facile ideas about glamour and sensation, as he did in "Young Sánchez." A note of harsh realism is struck at the close of section 11 when a boxer is told bluntly that he must finish a gruelling fight if he wants to continue making a living. Section 13 then exposes the abject poverty and neglect which even a one-time champion may suffer, before he eventually receives a crude and undistinguished burial.

On the more positive side, Aldecoa evokes qualities of heroism and grandeur by referring to classical literature, in particular to the triumphal odes of the Greek poets Simonides and Pindar, and on four occasions to the Latin satirist Gaius Lucilius. Eight of the fourteen sections are introduced briefly by loose prose translations from these and other classical sources which identify contemporary boxing with the epic struggles of ancient history and mythology. The religious value which the Olympian and other games had for the Greeks is reflected in a playful compendium of prayers for use on various occasions in the ring, reminiscent of the request of heroes for strength and inspiration from their gods. Aldecoa momentarily draws on Ovid in his presentation of a boxer on the threshold of magnificence:

Ahora es crisálida de campeón. Crisálida amenazada por dos alas de hierro febril e insolidario. Los castigados puños han sido vendados, enguantados, animados a partir al combate, reclamados a la guardia, alzados en el largo camino victorioso de la metamorfosis. (sect. 6)

For now he is the chrysalis of a champion. A chrysalis threatened by two wings of restless inimical iron. His punished hands have been bandaged, gloved, encouraged to go out and fight, called back on guard, lifted up on the long, victorious road to metamorphosis.

Jupiter, Heracles, Achilles, Ulysses, and Polydeuces are all mentioned in the motifs, while the name of Narcissus is pitilessly applied to a boxer who, on the morning after a dour title fight, refuses to believe that the disfigured face pictured on a sports page is his own. Such resonances and analogies serve as a point of reference for expressing both the glory and the tragedy of boxing.

Typical of Aldecoa's style are the passages of terse dialogue and patterned narrative, his descriptions of atmosphere and setting, and above all his recourse to imagery as seen in the following examples: "El campeón descansa sus puños entreabiertos, bostezantes, sobre sus rodillas" ("The champion rests his fists half open, yawning, on his knees," sect. 1); "Su bata encarnada ... era una llama huída del infierno envolviendo a un demonio" ("His red robe ... was a flame escaping from hell, wrapped around a demon," sect. 7); "Las sombras de los boxeadores son sombras de callejón sin salida, de cuento infantil que da miedo, de desván con objetos viejos y amputados..." ("Boxers' shadows are shadows found in blind alleys, in frightening children's tales, in attics full of old, dismembered objects..." sect. 4). While *Neutral Corner* exemplifies many of the essential characteristics of Aldecoa's work, it is an original experiment which still awaits definitive critical assessment.

CHAPTER 12

Exercises in Poetry

B EFORE establishing himself as a writer of fiction Aldecoa had
already published two volumes of poems. He was to register his
predilection for poetry in one of his many declarations to the press:
"Poetry has always commanded my greatest admiration."[1] He
regarded it as the quintessential form of literary expression. But it
was not a standard by which he wanted to be judged, and he would
describe himself simply as "a poet of imitations."

Aldecoa's published poems number only forty-five, and his
achievements in the genre on the whole bear out his modest denial
of originality. For the purpose of classification it is possible to identify him in the context of Spanish poetry in the 1940s with those
poets of the Generation of 1936 whose work was romantic in
theme, lyrical and intimate in tone, and marked by a return to
classical forms. During the last years of the Republic poets like Luis
Felipe Vivanco, Leopoldo Panero, Luis Rosales, Dionisio
Ridruejo, and Germán Bleiberg had found inspiration in the
sixteenth-century lyric poet Garcilaso de la Vega. *Garcilasismo* was
carried over into the years 1940–1946, but in a form debased and
stultified by the values of the new regime. This second wave of
garcilasista poetry has been dismissed consistently as insipid, facile,
and escapist. While admitting Aldecoa's inevitable subjection to
the constraints and influences operating in the post–Civil War
period, it is with the spirit, though not with the achievements, of
the first wave that we can best identify his poetry. In deference to
his disavowal of pretensions, it is also as a craftsman in the medium
of verse — rhythm, arrangement, and figuration — that Aldecoa's
talent may in part be assessed.

I Todavía la vida

Todavía la vida (*Life Still Goes on*)[2] is a collection of nineteen

144

sonnets written in a variety of styles. The first three poems are careful imitations of the mystical manner of Saint John of the Cross and Saint Teresa of Avila, two outstanding figures in sixteenth-century Spanish letters. The poems are most certainly exercises in literary technique, since spiritual and religious problems were far from Aldecoa's concern. His skillful handling of the rhetoric and imagery of the archetype compensates to a great degree for the inevitable depreciation of lyric sensibility. Poem 1 is an exceedingly morbid evocation of suffering: "Siete negros gorgojos por la aorta ... / Mis siete brechas padeciendo el alma" ("Seven gobs of blood rise from the aorta ... / My soul suffers from seven wounds," 7). The poet identifies with the Virgin Mary of Seven Sorrows, pleading for divine attention and reiterating his grief. An image of persecution: "el negro carro de mis siete estrellas" ("the black carriage of my seven stars"), calls to mind the fatalistic vision of Miguel Hernández, whose influence may be seen in the poem's graphic vocabulary and in the chiasmus, repetition, and symmetry of the following line in Spanish: "sangrando acero y mi voluntad sangrando." Poem 2 expresses the theme of man's desire to transcend the physical world and attain communion with God. The poet is poised in an intermediate state:

> Entre ti y lo que hiciste, suspendido,
> amándote sin freno ni cordura.
> . . . .
> Queriéndome volar y a ti volando.

> Suspended between you and your creation,
> Loving you without restraint or common sense.
> . . . .
> Wanting to fly and flying toward you.

The final tercet echoes Saint John of the Cross' famous oxymoron:

> Vivo sin vivir en mi,
> y de tal manera espero
> que muero porque no muero.

> I live and do not live in myself,
> and so strong are my hopes
> that I am dying of not dying.

The imaginary fulfillment of a mystical experience is described in poem 3, which opens with a frenzied plea for consolation and possession and closes at the moment of imminent surrender of the self. Patterns of alliteration, assonance, and antithetical imagery (fire-ice, sight-blindness) make this poem a particularly complex technical achievement.

The next six sonnets are inspired by friendship. In one Aldecoa celebrates the wisdom, ingenuity, and poetic skills of Carlos Edmundo de Ory, with the absurd exuberance and challenging metaphors characteristic of the *postistas:*

> ¿Quién te ha roto el ombligo y en qué poro
> de tu Himalaya te guardaste amante?
> ¿Quién te ha dado la hormiga y el sextante
> para medir tu verso y tu tesoro? (14)

> Who has opened up your stomach and in which pore
> of your Himalayan figure did you keep your love?
> Who has given you the ant and the sextant
> to measure your verse and your treasure?

There is an overall unity of imagery and sentiment in the other five poems. The poet expresses his nostalgia and regret over the absence or departure of close companions, through allusions to the sea and tides, and to beaches, rocks, and boats. There is a pleasing simplicity in intimations like "Yo, acaso, tan viejo porque dudo / que vuelvas con las nubes y las velas" ("I feel so old, perhaps, because I doubt / that you will ever return with the clouds and the sails," 19), and

> El mundo es tan pequeño, tan pequeño
> que todo él cabe en un pequeño sueño
> mientras viva el amigo y el hermano. (20)

> The world is so small, so small
> that it fits perfectly into a small dream
> as long as friend and brother exist.

Aldecoa next devotes three sonnets to the plains, mountains, and coastline of the Basque country. His pastoral vision has a distinctly literary basis, as the description of an afternoon setting as "Vergilian" shows. Though marred by a regrettable abuse of adjectives which renders the evocation of natural beauty over-indulgent, these poems avoid preciosity by extolling the robust, heroic spirit of the Basques in the manner of Ramón de Basterra, a native of Bilbao whose imposing verse appeared in the second decade of this century. The rugged coast thunders "un himno de la raza, bravío y navegante" ("a hymn for the race, wild and seafaring") and "una canción de hierro en una voz de atalante" ("a song of steel sung by Atalante"). Aldecoa chooses the line of fourteen syllables, in preference to the hendecasyllables used elsewhere in *Life Still Goes on*, for the possibilities it affords of expansive, majestic rhythms corresponding to the epic mood.

The sea is again a source of admiration, delight, and sometimes fear, in three sonnets "desde cubierta" ("from on deck"). A major criticism could be advanced, that Aldecoa does no more than paint sensitive and ornate word-pictures, without achieving an authentic interiorization of the landscape. Also, similes too often play the part properly reserved for imagery. The poems nevertheless contain occasional felicitous metaphors, as when "La popa ... su blanco encaje / teje en la estela que desaparece" ("The stern weaves its white lace / patterns in the disappearing wake," 31) and "La ola del horizonte muere en ciega / lucha de sueño con la tarde incierta" ("The last wave on the horizon dies in a blind / and sleepy struggle with the uncertain evening," 32).

One critic has suggested that the poems in *Life Still Goes on* are united by a common spirit of youthful delight in life's pleasures.[3] At first sight the three Anachreontic "Versos del vino alegre" ("Verses on the Joys of Wine") would appear to substantiate this opinion, for they personify drink as a faithful friend or expert lover. But the idea of death is also present, notably in the third poem whose meaning rests on an analogy between the poet's life and the decline of day. At sunset the sky takes on the deep red color of wine and blood, as if it were a wounded bull. Although the poet acknowledges this symbolic reminder of his own mortality, he refuses to renounce the fatal pleasure of drinking the juice of the vine

> en donde liba
> el ocaso su fuerza y su contento,
> aunque luego mi ocaso sea luego. (39)

> wherein
> the dying day finds strength and satisfaction,
> even though it eventually be the death of me.

In the concluding sonnet of this collection Aldecoa describes the course of a stream which flows from a mysterious mountain source down to the sea, "el amado ... / salmo de salmos donde todo queda" ("the beloved ... / psalm of psalms where everything comes to rest," 43). His perception of the cosmic spirit running through the whole of nature resembles the pantheistic vision of Juan Ramón Jiménez.

Life Still Goes on is a poet's apprenticeship. On its appearance Leopoldo de Luis hailed "a poetic temperament, intense and clearly defined."[4] Many of Aldecoa's images are indeed clear evidence of poetic sensitivity and vision. Clumsiness in style and prosody detracts only occasionally from his imaginative powers of expression, his resourceful use of figures of speech, and his sure sense of poetic arrangement.

II   Libro de las algas

Libro de las algas (*Book of the Algae*),[5] published in 1949, consists of twenty-six poems loosely united by themes and imagery of the sea. One, pictorial type represents maritime scenes including the activities of sailors and fishermen. A second, symbolic type uses images of the sea to express themes of time and love. Lastly, three obscure poems entitled "Tentaciones" ("Temptations") capture the mysterious atmosphere of night time.

The lyrical spirit of Rafael Alberti in *Marinero en Tierra* (*Sailor on Land*) is present throughout the volume, especially in the lament

> En la tierra no soy más
> que una triste alga perdida
> sobre el triste esqueleto de la orilla. (27)

> On land I am nothing more
> than a sad and lost piece of seaweed
> on the sad outline of the shore.

The poet celebrates the physical, almost sexual, exhilaration which sailing can provide:

> los marineros
> abren las venas de las olas.
>
> . . . .
> la quilla sabe

de las primicias de las bodas. (15)

the sailors
open up veins in the waves.
. . . .
the keel knows all
about the first fruits of marriage.

He records the fear and respect inspired by the sea: "cementerio de gaviotas y de olas, / manicomio de barcos perdidos" ("a graveyard of gulls and waves, a madhouse of ships off course," 11). He witnesses elements of religion and lore in the sailors' attitudes:

Allá, donde las aves
se petrifican en el aire,
bajan alborotados en las nieblas
los ángeles custodios de la nave. (43)

In the distance, where the birds
turn to stone in the air,
the angels who watch over ships
come down excitedly in the mists.

Personification of ships is common, as in the early story "Biography of a Figurehead" and passages describing the *Chipirrín* in *Part of a Story*. Aldecoa also draws on a general mythology of the sea which includes references to a flood, an ark, and many other motifs. Poem 5 of section 1 exemplifies both these procedures:

Tu armadura, hecha añicos
danza sobre tu carne tronadora
guerrero de los arcos infinitos.

Ciego diamante el día,
medusa muerta el sol
florecen en tu barba de ventiscas.

A veces, un viejo y bello santo,
dormido en la penumbra de los hielos,
misionero de siglos lejanos;
a veces, un errante fantasma,
forjador de los vientos,
en líquidas fraguas;
a veces, una blanca leyenda
de los hombres del norte
que sueñan.

A veces eres todo; a veces sólo
agua azul, viento azul,
pupilas de osos.

A veces eres todo, blanco guerrero anciano
que tienes sepultado
tu corazón en Malstrom.   (12)

Your armor, smashed to pieces,
dances on your thundering flesh,
warrior of infinite bows.

A blind diamond the day,
a dead jellyfish the sun,
flourish in your beard of blizzards.

Sometimes, an old and beautiful saint,
asleep in the shadow of masses of ice,
a missionary from distant centuries;
sometimes, a wandering phantom,
hammering the winds
in liquid forges;
sometimes, a white legend
for the men of the north
who dream.

Sometimes you are everything; sometimes only
blue water, blue wind,
the eyeballs of polar bears.

Sometimes you are everything, ancient white warrior,
whose heart is buried
in Maelstrom.

The poet fondly apostrophizes a broken hulk as if it were an ancient warrior. This technique of personification extends throughout the poem, which may be divided into three balanced sections of six, nine, and six lines each. In stanza 1 a metaphorical reference to the warrior's "thundering" flesh beneath his armor renders the boat's vigorous resistance to the noisy waves which batter against it. A drift of pale sand in which the prow of the vessel is lying becomes a snowy white beard on the hero's face. It catches the sun's reflection, which is round and colorless like a dead jellyfish washed up against the hulk. The poem's central section conjures up an imaginary and mythical past, in which the warrior assumes the guises of first, a Christian missionary or crusader, and second, a wandering phantom. There is an echo here of the legend of the Flying Dutchman. A Greek myth, that of the Cyclops who forged thunderbolts for Zeus, inspires the metaphor of the warrior-forger in lines 11 and 12. A third connection with mythology and lore is suggested in the final tercet of this section: in his mysterious past the warrior may have figured in the legends of that Northern race of bellicose seafarers, the Vikings. The remote North is again evoked in the last two stanzas. Converging on the horizon, sea and sky are two blue specks like a polar bear's eyes. Another image has it that the warrior's heart is buried in the notorious Maelstrom whirlpool. The poem derives most of its imaginative and emotive appeal from the sustained practice of personification and cultivation of epic resonances.

On other occasions the sea is seen as a symbol of various aspects of human experience, in particular of temporality and love. Imagery thus ceases to have a merely ornamental function, as may be seen in the following poem entitled "Retratos" ("Portraits"):

> La angustia de los ácidos retratos,
> membrillos en el polvo de los años,
> vierte por la consola un débil rayo
> de momentos robados.
>
> Una vida nos brinda su noticia
> en unos ojos secos contenida
> y el arco estrangulado de la risa
> su alma arrugada fija.
>
> El mar de los retratos, el mar pleno,
> amor de los marineros en el viento,
> un estanque podrido por el tiempo,
> un estanque, parece, fijo y muerto. (32)

> The anguish of acid portraits,
> quince fruits in the dust of years,
> casts over the console a weak ray
> of stolen moments.
>
> A life tells us its news
> contained in dry eyes,
> and the strangled arch of laughter
> fixes its crumpled soul.
>
> The sea of portraits, the sea in swell,
> the love of sailors in the wind,

> looks like a pool stagnant long ago,
> a pool motionless and dead.

The poem comprises two clusters of images: those deriving from the poet's intuition that a picture's material properties — color, size, texture — are consubstantial with the scene it represents; and those references to sea and water which appear in the last strophe. At the start, old pictures are seen as symbolizing the ephemerality of human life. Canvas and paper are liable to fade and decay, and the moment of human experience which an artist tries to capture is thus destroyed. The poet is afflicted with anguish which he projects onto the object of his attention. Looking at pictures brings a sour taste to his mouth, and his poetic imagination transforms them into bitter fruits. He comments on one particular portrait which is dry and crumpled: the face it represents is accordingly wizened and disfigured, since a crease in the paper has twisted the person's mouth into an expression of death. This grimace is, in turn, the outward sign of a "crumpled" soul. The unexpected metaphor of "the sea of portraits" gives emphasis to the ideas of transience and death. A stagnant pool becomes a poetic correlative for deterioration and decay, set in contrast to the open sea whose plenitude is a symbol of vitality. The division of line 12 into three segments of four, three, and four syllables, with asymmetrical stress on the eighth and tenth, reinforces the poem's depressing message.

The theme of frustrated love appears in three narrative poems, each with the title of "Huellas" ("Footprints"). In a stylized setting of deserted beaches swept by autumnal winds, the poet laments the loss of his loved one. The following poem is the second in the trilogy:

> Viniste con el viento del norte
> y las estrellas fugaces;
> como éstas, viniste
> un momento, sin duda,
> con una nueva y ensayada huída
> batiendo la vela del recuerdo.
>
> Viniste, metálica y erguida,
> con un licor de espumas en los labios
> y un verano dormido en grises playas.
>
> Azul vorágine de yolas,
> de chimeneas altas, de esperanzas,

te brotaba en la risa.

Otra vez los barcos se mudaban
por un oceáno latino y afectado;
otra vez los párpados traviesos,
fingían los reflejos de las aguas.

Otra vez, como siempre
como una estrella navegante
te fuiste a naufragar con las gaviotas. (39)

You came with the north wind
and shooting stars;
no doubt, you came
like these one moment,
in a new and rehearsed escape
shaking memory's canvas sail.

You came, metallic and upright,
with foaming liquor on your lips
and a sleepy summer on grey beaches.

A blue whirlpool of yawls,
tall chimneys and hopes
erupted in your smile.

Once again the boats were off
across a Latin, affected sea;
once again mischievous eyes
copied reflections in the water.

Once again, as always
like a seafaring star
you headed for a shipwreck with the gulls.

Images of ships on the move convey the transience of human relations. The woman arrived like a ship whose sail is an emblem of memory, and sails away to destruction in a shipwreck which symbolizes failure in love. She is associated with wind, birds, and the rhythms of nature. Her movements are arbitrary like those of a shooting star, beyond human understanding. She has the sensuous charm of the sea: her lips sting with the taste of brine, and her blue eyes are tempestuous whirlpools. Nature imagery thus renders the poet's private experience in universal terms.

Alliteration, tripartite formal schemes, and variation in the verse form are an integral part of the poem's effect. The repetition of *v*, *n,* and *t* sounds in line 1 establishes a sense of melancholy. A similar mood derives from the plaintive reiteration of "viniste" in the final part of the poem. In the second, repetition of the emphatically placed phrase "otra vez" brings out the inevitability of the woman's departure. The measured accumulation of syllables in the last three lines is a figure for her disappearance, and the poet's fall into despondency is also mirrored in this rhythmic structure.

III   *Conclusion*

Book of the Algae consolidates Aldecoa's reputation as a writer of lyrical gifts and subtle perceptions. It must be admitted that the quality of emotion in his poetry does not reach the levels of tension and passion exemplified in the work of Jiménez, Lorca, or Hernández. Nor does his imagination compare in scope with Aleixandre's. Aldecoa's poetry is nevertheless a coherent projection of his thoughts and feelings, in a personal language which is rich in expressive resources and associations.

CHAPTER 13

Conclusion

I GNACIO Aldecoa was acclaimed as a writer of distinct promise upon the publication of his first works, and continued to arouse critical interest up to and after his death. His commentators have voiced varied and, on balance, favorable opinions about his work. While adverse criticism has sometimes been founded on misunderstanding or prejudice, certain charges cannot be refuted. At the outset Aldecoa tended toward technical virtuosity and excessive elaborateness in style. Some critics hold that refusal to make concessions to his readers is a persistent fault, since the complexity of his writing militates against its comprehension by a wide public. As far as particular works are concerned, two volumes of stories, *Birds and Scarecrows* and *Archaeology,* are undeniably mediocre in their concerted effect and have done little to enhance Aldecoa's reputation. We must also acknowledge the limitations of his poetry, as the author himself did.

Such reservations are counterbalanced by the ready acceptance of the solid ethical and artistic foundations of Aldecoa's literary world. Based on a commitment to human justice and solidarity with his fellowman, Aldecoa's work leaves a lasting impression of sincerity and authenticity. This is due both to the compelling accuracy with which he describes conditions in Spain in the contemporary period, and to the integrity of his artistic creed. Aldecoa was radically independent of prevailing cultural groups and trends. He remained faithful to his declared ambitions, as outlined in chapter 2 of this study, and developed consistently to creative maturity. His work throughout was inspired by unchanging social and existential preoccupations and a constant aspiration toward technical perfection.

The themes expressed in the novels and stories make up a personal ideology or world view with an appeal and relevance beyond the boundaries of Spain. According to this view, chance and fate

155

determine the course of human destiny so that life is ultimately a gamble against the odds; personal freedom is constrained by arbitrary forces of nature and society, and by moral values operating in an inconsistent, even gratuitous way. Such a pessimistic response faithfully reflects the sensibility of modern man who inhabits a world of conflict and crisis. Aldecoa, who owed a debt to foreign authors, was thus able to repay it through a personal contribution to the corpus of world literature. Translation of his work into at least eight languages, including German, Polish, and Japanese, has rendered it accessible to readers in Western and Central Europe, the American continent, and elsewhere.

As regards Aldecoa's relation to a developing literary tradition, we may note how he constructively reappraised accepted conventions and judiciously experimented with new ones. This is true in the two respects of genre and technique. Of particular significance is Aldecoa's inclination for the parable and, to a lesser extent, the fable. Like Muriel Spark and William Golding, Aldecoa turned to allegorical types to treat the moral dilemmas of modern man. As we have seen, he found the conceptual framework of the sea narrative conducive to articulating his world view. Aldecoa updated the conventions of naturalist realism and modified the particularly Spanish tradition of the *esperpento* to suit changed circumstances. His reappraisal of costumbrism and critique of tremendism were major conditions of the reform of Spanish prose fiction in the 1950s. The "neo-realist" mode provided a profoundly human perspective with which to combat the alleged parochialism and mediocrity of much of recent Spanish fiction. Aldecoa was also able to judge contemporary society through exuberant satires, caricatures, and conceits adapted from Quevedo and Valle-Inclán with an unerring sense of relevance.

His experiments in form and narrative technique place Aldecoa at the center of the modern movement which revalues inherited artistic norms. He chose to parody conventions of plot and suspense in *Blood and Lightning,* to trim and simplify narrative structure in *Great Sole* and "Young Sánchez," and to transcend realistic conventions of language, character, and setting in "Bird of Paradise." He experimented with an objective mode of presentation but found it unsuited to his anthropomorphic concerns. Through interior duplication he explored the codes and conventions of fiction in a genuine attempt to discover adequate means of symbolic expression. While his fiction is distinctly modern, Aldecoa did not pursue modernity for its own sake but subordinated innovation to the goal of achieving organic unity in each of his works.

In the singularity of his moral purpose, in his fidelity to artistic criteria, and in his professional appreciation of his craft, Aldecoa stands as an example to writers of future generations. His influence as a novelist will depend on general recognition of the historical, philosophical, and artistic value of *With the East Wind, Great Sole,* and *Part of a Story.* As a writer of short stories he is already an acknowledged master in Spain. Many of his narratives record for posterity the intimate dilemmas of contemporary man in a developing industrial society; others treat themes of universal and permanent significance. Although Spain lost an authentic literary presence when Ignacio Aldecoa died, it acquired a finished and coherent body of work for its cultural tradition.

Notes and References

Chapter One

1. When interviewed in *El Español* (20–26 March 1955), 45–48.
2. Luis de Sastre, "La vuelta de Ignacio Aldecoa," *La Estafeta Literaria* 169 (15 May 1959), 23.
3. In his book *Ignacio Aldecoa* (Madrid: Espesa, 1972), pp. 29–30.
4. In an introduction to Aldecoa's *Cuentos,* ed. Josefina Rodríguez de Aldecoa (Madrid: Cátedra, 1977), p. 13.
5. "¿Por qué gritan los mayores? Vago recuerdo del S.E.U. en el Instituto," *La Hora* 71 (26 November 1950), 9.
9. In "Anécdota particular y nostálgica," *La Hora, número extraordinario,* 24 June 1950, p. 38.
7. In her prolog to *La tierra de nadie y otros relatos* by Ignacio Aldecoa (Barcelona: Salvat, 1970), p. 9.
8. Ramón Tamames, *La República La Era de Franco,* 5th ed. (Madrid: Alfaguara, 1976), p. 508.
9. Salvador Giner, "Power, Freedom and Social Change in the Spanish University, 1939–1975," in *Spain in Crisis: The Evolution and Decline of the Franco Regime,* ed. Paul Preston (London: Harvester, 1976), p. 184.
10. Ibid., p. 185.
11. Carmen Martín Gaite, "Un aviso: ha muerto Ignacio Aldecoa," *La Estafeta Literaria* 433 (1 December 1969), 4–7.
12. Jesús Fernández Santos, "Ignacio y yo," *Insula* 280 (March 1970), 11.
13. See his *Poesía 1945–1969,* ed. Félix Grande (Barcelona: Edhasa, 1970), p. 273.
14. In "Carta de un estudiante a otro estudiante sobre materia postista," *El Español* 188 (1 June 1946), 3.
15. José María Martínez Cachero, "Ignacio Aldecoa: 'Seguir de pobres,' " in *El comentario de textos,* no. 2 (Madrid: Castalia, 1974), pp. 211–12.
16. Gómez de la Serna, "Un estudio sobre la literatura social de Ignacio Aldecoa," in *Ensayos sobre literatura social* (Madrid: Guadarrama, 1971), p. 88.
17. See Lorenzo Gomis, "Pesca de altura. *Gran Sol* de Ignacio Aldecoa," *El Ciervo* 7, no. 63 (March 1958), 6, and Baltasar Porcel Pujol,

"Una novela del mar," *Papeles de Son Armadans* 9, no. 26 (May 1958), 235–36.

18. Luis Sastre, "La vuelta de Ignacio Aldecoa," p. 24.

19. In his article "Two Representatives of the Rising Young Generation of Spanish Novelists: José Luis Castillo Puche and Ignacio Aldecoa," *Kentucky Foreign Language Quarterly,* 7, no. 2 (1960), 86.

20. During an interview for the magazine *Griffith,* 3 December 1965, p. 8.

21. "Hablando de *Escuadra hacia la muerte,*" *Revista Española* 1 (May–June 1953), 119.

22. Francisco García Pavón, "Semblanzas españolas: Ignacio Aldecoa novelista, cuentista," *Indice de Artes y Letras* 146 (February 1961), 4.

23. See her edition of Aldecoa's *Cuentos completos,* 2 vols. (Madrid: Alianza, 1973), I, 10.

24. Declarations for *La Nación,* 20 April 1969.

25. Dionisio Ridruejo, "Presencia de Ignacio Aldecoa," *Destino* 35, no. 184 (14 April 1973), 41.

26. In "Poco más que anécdotas 'culturales' alrededor de quince años (1950–1965)," *Triunfo, número extraordinario* 507 (17 June 1972), 82.

27. Ridruejo, "Presencia de Ignacio Aldecoa," p. 41.

28. These comments appear in *Griffith,* 3 December 1965, p. 7..

29. Fernández Santos, "Ignacio y yo," p. 11, and García Luengo, "Una tarde con Ignacio Aldecoa," *El Urogallo,* no. 0 (December 1969), 20–22.

30. When interviewed by Alvaro Linares Rivas for *Crítica,* 4 January 1958.

Chapter Two

1. Sebejano, *Novela española de nuestro tiempo* (Madrid: Prensa Española, p. 16.

2. Rubio, *Narrativa española 1940–1970* (Madrid: Epesa, 1970), p. 22.

3. Anonymous, "Ignacio Aldecoa: programa para largo," *Destino* 956 (3 December 1955), 37.

4. Luis de Sastre, "La vuelta de Ignacio Aldecoa," p. 24.

5. B. "Preguntas a Ignacio Aldecoa," *Indice de Artes y Letras* 132 (December 1959), 4.

6. Anon., "Ignacio Aldecoa: programa para largo," p. 37.

7. Miguel Fernández Braso, "Ignacio Aldecoa levanta acta de los *Años de crisálida,*" *Indice de Artes y Letras* 236 (October 1968), 42.

8. Gil Casado, *La novela social española (1942–1968)* (Barcelona: Seix Barral, 1968), p. viii.

9. Sobejano, *Novela española de nuestro tiempo,* p. 418.

10. Cited by Josefina Rodríguez de Aldecoa in *Cuentos,* p. 38.

11. Corrales Egea, *La novela española actual* (Madrid: Cuadernos para el Diálogo, 1971), pp. 126–32.

12. Schwartz, *Spain's New Wave Novelists 1950–1974* (Metuchen, N.J.: Scarecrow, 1976), p. 16.

13. Anon., "La novela en baja forma," *Correo Literario* 64 (15 January 1953), 9.

14. In "El arte de novelar," *Cuadernos Hispanoamericanos* 45 (September 1953), 401.

15. Donald L. Shaw, *A Literary History of Spain: The Nineteenth Century* (London: Ernest Benn, 1972), p. 20.

16. Miguel de Santiago, "Ignacio Aldecoa: una historia partida   Entrevista con Josefina Rodríguez," *La Estafeta Literaria* 578 (15 December 1975), 8.

17. Anon. "Ignacio Aldecoa: programa para largo," p. 37.

18. Borau, *El existencialismo en la novela de Ignacio Aldecoa* (Zaragoza: Talleres Gráficos "La Editorial", 1974), p. 20.

19. Grupp, "Two Representatives of the Rising Young Generation of Spanish Novelists...," p. 85, and Gómez de la Serna, "Un estudio sobre la literatura social de Ignacio Aldecoa," pp. 72, 135.

20. Navales, *Cuatro novelistas españoles: M. Delibes, I. Aldecoa, D. Sueiro, F. Umbral* (Madrid: Fundamentos, 1974), p. 112.

21. Esteban Soler, "Narradores españoles del Medio Siglo," in *Miscellanea di studi ispanici* (Pisa: University of Pisa, 1971–1973), pp. 217–370.

22. Eugenio de Nora, *La novela española contemporánea,* 3 vols. (Madrid: Gredos, 1962), III, 259–328; Julio Martínez de la Rosa, "Notas para un estudio sobre Ignacio Aldecoa," *Cuadernos Hispanoamericanos* 241 (January 1970), 188–89; Darío Villanueva, *"El Jarama" de Sánchez Ferlosio Su estructura y significado* (Santiago: University of Santiago of Compostela, 1973), pp. 21–35; and García Viñó, *Ignacio Aldecoa,* pp. 14–15.

23. See the report of Aldecoa's lecture, "Panorama particular de la narrativa española de hoy," in *El Día* (Santa Cruz de Tenerife), 4 March 1961, p. 7.

24. In Luis Sastre, "La vuelta de Ignacio Aldecoa," p. 23.

25. José María de Quinto, "Lo intimista en la literatura social," *Correo Literario* 61 (1 December 1952), 3.

26. García Pavón, "Ignacio Aldecoa, novelista, cuentista," p. 4.

27. Gómez de la Serna, "Un estudio sobre la literatura social de Ignacio Aldecoa," p. 112.

28. In his declarations to *Griffith,* 3 December 1965, p. 6.

29. Fernández Braso, "Ignacio Aldecoa levanta acta de los *Años de crisálida,*" p. 42.

30. See Harold Reynolds, "Archetypal Perception in Rafael Sánchez Ferlosio's *Alfanhui,*" *Bulletin of Hispanic Studies* 53, no. 3 (July 1976),

162   IGNACIO ALDECOA

215–24, and Francisco García Sarriá, *"El Jarama.* Muerte y merienda de Lucita," *Bulletin of Hispanic Studies* 53, no. 4 (October 1976), 323–37.

31. See Margaret W. Jones, "Religious and Biblical Material in the Works of Ana María Matute," *Hispania* 51, no. 3 (1968), 416–23.

32. B., "Preguntas a Ignacio Aldecoa," p. 4.

33. Luis Sastre, "La vuelta de Ignacio Aldecoa," p. 24.

34. Cited by Josefina Rodríguez de Aldecoa in *Cuentos,* p. 34.

35. A declaration to Jorge del Corral of *Teleradio* 621 (17–23 November 1969), 56.

36. B., "Preguntas a Ignacio Aldecoa," p. 4.

37. Luis Sastre, "La vuelta de Ignacio Aldecoa," p. 23.

38. Manuel García Viñó, *Ignacio Aldecoa,* p. 66.

39. B., "Preguntas a Ignacio Aldecoa," p. 4.

40. Martínez de la Rosa, "Notas para un estudio sobre Ignacio Aldecoa," p. 193.

41. Luis Sastre, "La vuelta de Ignacio Aldecoa," p. 23.

42. Ibid., p. 24.

43. José Julio Perlado, "Ignacio Aldecoa escribe *Parte de una historia,"* *El Alcázar,* 3 May 1967, p. 21.

44. In conversation with Julio Trenas of *Pueblo,* 6 October 1956.

45. Burns, *Doce cuentistas españoles de la posguerra* (London: Harrap, 1968), pp. 18–20, and Brandenberger, *Estudios sobre el cuento español actual* (Madrid: Editora Nacional, 1973), pp. 18–19.

46. Ana María Matute, "The Short Story in Spain," trans. William Fifield, *Kenyon Review* 31 (April 1969), 450–54.

47. Fraile, "Panorama del cuento contemporáneo en España," *Cahiers du Monde Hispanique et Luso-Brésilien (Caravelle)* 17 (1971), 170.

48. Hierro, "El cuento, como género literario," *Cuadernos Hispanoamericanos* 61 (January 1955), 60–66.

49. José Julio Perlado, "Ignacio Aldecoa escribe *Parte de una historia,"* p. 21.

50. See "El cuento en los Estados Unidos," in Aldecoa's private papers.

51. Cited by Josefina Rodríguez de Aldecoa in *Cuentos,* p. 40.

52. Bergonzi, *Situation of the Novel* (London: Macmillan, 1971), pp. 214–15.

53. Baquero Goyanes, *Antología de cuentos contemporáneos* (Barcelona: Labor, 1964), pp. xxvii–xxix.

54. Burns, *Doce cuentistas españoles de la posguerra,* p. 15.

Chapter Three

1. Fernández Braso, "Ignacio Aldecoa levanta acta de los *Años de crisálida,"* p. 42.

2. Corrales Egea, *La novela española actual (Ensayo de ordenación)*

(Madrid: Edicusa, 1971), pp. 128–30, and Sanz Villanueva, *Tendencias de la novela española actual* (Madrid: Edicusa, 1972), p. 176.

3. Ignacio Aldecoa, *El fulgor y la sangre*, 3d ed. (Barcelona: Ed. Planeta, 1970), p. 222; hereafter references are cited in the text.

4. Borau, *El existencialismo en la novela de Ignacio Aldecoa*, pp. 91–149.

5. Luis Sastre, "La vuelta de Ignacio Aldecoa," p. 24.

6. Eugenio de Nora, *La novela española contemporánea*, III, 304.

7. José María Castellet, "Veinte años de novela española (1942–1962)," *Indice de Artes y Letras* 173 (May 1963), p. 13, and Juan Carlos Curutchet, *Introducción a la novela española de posguerra* (Montevideo: Alfa, 1966), pp. 30–31, 58–59.

8. Castellet, An untitled essay in *Correo Literario* 6, no. 10 (February–March 1955), 33.

9. Pérez Firmat, "The Structure of *El fulgor y la sangre*," *Hispanic Review* 45, no. 1 (Winter 1977), 4–5.

10. Alborg, "Los novelistas: Ignacio Aldecoa," *Indice de Artes y Letras* 100–101 (April–May 1957), iv.

11. Pérez Firmat, "The Structure of *El fulgor y la sangre*," p. 6.

12. Ibid., p. 5.

13. Fernández Almagro, "*El fulgor y la sangre* por Ignacio Aldecoa," *ABC*, 3 April 1955, p. 51.

Chapter Four

1. Ignacio Aldecoa, *Con el viento solano*, 2d ed. (Barcelona: Ed. Planeta, 1962), p. 248; hereafter references are cited in the text.

2. Luis Sastre, "La vuelta de Ignacio Aldecoa," p. 24.

3. Eugenio de Nora, *La novela española contemporánea*, III, 305.

4. Bosch, *La novela española del siglo XX*, 2 vols. (New York: Las Américas, 1970), II, 143.

5. Sobejano, *Novela española de nuestro tiempo*, p. 301.

6. Janet Winecoff Díaz, "The Novels of Ignacio Aldecoa," *Romance Notes* 11, no. 3 (1969), 479.

7. Roberts, *Temas existenciales en la novela española de la posguerra* (Madrid: Gredos, 1973), pp. 99–128.

8. B., "Preguntas a Ignacio Aldecoa," p. 4.

9. Carlisle, "Amos and Haggai: Sources of Thematic Motif and Stylistic Form in Ignacio Aldecoa's *Con el viento solano*," *Bulletin of the Rocky Mountain Modern Language Association* 26 (Fall 1972), 83–84.

10. Borau, *El existencialismo en la novela de Ignacio Aldecoa*, pp. 23–31.

11. Sobejano, "Sobre el arte descriptivo de Ignacio Aldecoa: *Con el viento solano*," in *Ignacio Aldecoa: A Collection of Criticial Essays* (Laramie: University of Wyoming Press, 1977), p. 17.

164   IGNACIO ALDECOA

12. Abbott, "Ignacio Aldecoa and the Journey to Paradise (The Short Stories)," in *Ignacio Aldecoa — A Collection of Critical Essays*, pp. 59–68.

13. José Julio Perlado, "Ignacio Aldecoa escribe *Parte de una historia*," p. 21.

14. R. B. B., *Con el viento solano*," *Indice de Artes y Letras* 93 (September 1956), 20.

15. García Viñó, *Ignacio Aldecoa*, p. 100.

16. Sobejano, "Sobre el arte descriptivo de Ignacio Aldecoa: *Con el viento solano*," pp. 17–27.

17. Carlisle, "Amos and Haggai: Sources of Thematic Motif and Stylistic Form in Ignacio Aldecoa's *Con el viento solano*," p. 87.

18. García Viñó, *Ignacio Aldecoa*, p. 108.

19. Fernández Almagro, "*Con el viento solano* por Ignacio Aldecoa," *ABC*, 8 July 1956, p. 81, and Gortari, author of a review of *Con el viento solano* in *Nuestro Tiempo* 6, no. 33 (March 1957), 381.

20. Juan Luis Alborg, "Los novelistas: Ignacio Aldecoa," p. iv.

21. Nora, *La novela española contemporánea*, III, 306.

22. Ibid., p. 302.

Chapter Five

1. "Un mar de historias," a literary supplement of *Oficema* 7, no. 77 (December 1961).

2. Ignacio Aldecoa, *Gran Sol*, 3d ed. (Barcelona: Noguer, 1969), p. 159; hereafter references are cited in the text.

3. García Viñó, *Ignacio Aldecoa*, p. 113, and Fischer, "La tragedia humilde en la narrativa de Ignacio Aldecoa" (Ph.D. diss., University of Miami, 1971), pp. 50–52.

4. Gonzalo Sobejano, *Novela española de nuestro tiempo*, p. 302.

5. García Viñó, *Ignacio Aldecoa*, p. 111.

6. Herman Melville, *Moby Dick* (London: New English Library, 1961), p. 25.

7. Ibid., pp. 172, 188, 487.

8. As acknowledged by Jack B. Jelinski in his article "Ignacio Aldecoa: A Forgotten Master. A Critical Re-examination of *Gran Sol*," in *Ignacio Aldecoa — A Collection of Critical Essays*, pp. 41–47.

9. *Moby Dick*, p. 310.

10. Jelinski, "Ignacio Aldecoa: A Forgotten Master," p. 43.

11. Torrente Ballester, *Panorama de la novela española contemporánea* (Madrid: Guadarrama, 1961), p. 458. See also Ricardo Senabre, "La obra narrativa de Ignacio Aldecoa," *Papeles de Son Armadans* 15, no. 166 (1970), p. 12, and J. Villa Pastur, "*Gran Sol*," *Archivum* 7 (1957), 358–60.

12. Nora, *La novela española contemporánea,* III, 307.

13. García Viñó, *Ignacio Aldecoa,* p. 123.

14. Disclosed in his lecture "Panorama particular de la narrativa española de hoy," and reported in *El Día* (Santa Cruz de Tenerife), 4 March 1961, p. 7.

15. Julio Trenas, "Así trabaja Ignacio Aldecoa," *Pueblo,* 5 October 1957, p. 11.

16. Jelinski, "Ignacio Aldecoa: A Forgotten Master," p. 47.

Chapter Six

1. Janet Winecoff Díaz, "The Novels of Ignacio Aldecoa," *Romance Notes* 11, no. 3 (1969), 479.

2. Salvador, "La Palma y La Graciosa, sustancias novelescas," *Homenaje a Elías Serra Ráfols* 3 (1970), 297–314.

3. Ignacio Aldecoa, *Parte de una historia,* 2d ed. (Barcelona: Noguer, 1973), p. 105; hereafter references are cited in the text.

4. Ronald Schwartz, *Spain's New Wave Novelists 1950–1974,* p. 221.

5. García Viñó, *Ignacio Aldecoa,* p. 139.

6. José Julio Perlado, "Ignacio Aldecoa escribe *Parte de una historia,*" p. 21.

7. Ricardo Senabre, "La obra narrativa de Ignacio Aldecoa," p. 16.

8. Salvador, "La Palma y La Graciosa, sustancias novelescas," pp. 305, 307.

9. José Domingo, *"Parte de una historia: narrativa española,"* Insula 252 (November 1967), 4.

10. Ronald Schwartz, *Spain's New Wave Novelists 1950–1974,* p. 225.

11. Ibid., p. 221.

12. Pérez Minik, *Entrada y salida de viajeros* (Santa Cruz de Tenerife: Ediciones Nuestro Arte, 1969), p. 95.

13. Carlisle, *Ecos del viento, silencios del mar: La novelística de Ignacio Aldecoa* (Madrid: Playor, 1976), p. 141.

Chapter Seven

1. Ignacio Aldecoa, *Cuentos completos,* ed. Alicia Bleiberg, 2 vols. (Madrid: Alianza, 1973), II, 273. In our analyses of stories in this and the next three chapters, references will be cited in the text.

2. Erna Brandenberger, *Estudios sobre el cuento español actual,* p. 154.

3. Espadas, "Técnica literaria y fondo social del cuento 'A ti no te enterramos' de Ignacio Aldecoa," *Papeles de Son Armadans,* nos. 245–46 (August–September 1976), 172.

4. Anonymous, "Ignacio Aldecoa: programa para largo," p. 37.
5. Abbott, "Ignacio Aldecoa and the Journey to Paradise (The Short Stories)," p. 59.
6. Anonymous, "Ignacio Aldecoa: programa para largo," p. 37.
7. Tudela, "Reflexiones ante dos libros de narraciones," *Cuadernos Hispanoamericanos* 70 (October 1955), 116.
8. Garciasol, *"Vísperas del silencio,"* Insula 115 (July 1955), 7.

Chapter Eight

1. In her edition of Aldecoa's *Cuentos completos,* p. 255.
2. Marra López, *"El corazón y otros frutos amargos,"* Insula 156 (November 1959), 6.
3. Erna Brandenberger remarks on the architecture of this story in her *Estudios sobre el cuento español actual,* pp. 188–91.
4. Urrutia, "Análisis de un cuento de Ignacio Aldecoa (Búsqueda de su 'primera lectura')," *Boletín de la Asociación Europea de Profesores de Español* 8, no. 14 (March 1967), 39–47.

Chapter Nine

1. Brandenberger, *Estudios sobre el cuento español actual,* pp. 226–27.
2. Anon., A Review of *Pájaros y espantapájaros, Cuadernos Hispanoamericanos* 175–76 (July–August 1964), 295.

Chapter Ten

1. Marra López, "Lirismo y esperpento en la obra de Ignacio Aldecoa," *Insula* 226 (September 1965), 5.
2. Brandenberger, *Estudios sobre el cuento español actual,* pp. 165–72.
3. Gómez de la Serna, "Un estudio sobre la literatura social de Ignacio Aldecoa," pp. 100–01.
4. García Viñó, *Ignacio Aldecoa,* p. 164.
5. See Fernando Guillermo de Castro, "Ignacio Aldecoa entre el alcohol y el mar," *Indice de Artes y Letras* 260 (15 December 1969), 28–30.
6. Janet Winecoff Díaz, "Amadís Existentialized: A Posthumous Tale by Ignacio Aldecoa," in *Ignacio Aldecoa — A Collection of Critical Essays,* p. 104.

Chapter Eleven

1. Gómez de la Serna, "Un estudio sobre la literatura social de Ignacio Aldecoa," pp. 156, 158.

2. Ignacio Aldecoa, *Cuaderno de godo* (Madrid: Arion, 1961), p. 13; hereafter references are cited in the text.

3. Ignacio Aldecoa, *El país vasco* (Barcelona: Noguer, 1962), p. 6; hereafter references are cited in the text.

4. Ignacio Aldecoa, *Neutral Corner* (Barcelona: Lumen, 1962); hereafter references are cited in the text.

5. Brandenberger, *Estudios sobre el cuento español actual,* p. 66.

Chapter Twelve

1. In an interview with Julio Trenas, "Así trabaja Ignacio Aldecoa," p. 11.

2. Ignacio Aldecoa, *Todavía la vida* (Madrid: Talleres Gráficos Argos, 1947); hereafter references are cited in the text.

3. Leopoldo de Luis, reviewing *Todavía la vida* in *Insula* 3, no. 30 (15 June 1948), iv.

4. Ibid., p. iv.

5. Ignacio Aldecoa, *Libro de las algas* (Madrid: Talleres Gráficos CIES, 1949); hereafter references are cited in the text.

Selected Bibliography

PRIMARY SOURCES

1. Books

Arqueología. Barcelona: Editorial Rocas, 1961.
Caballo de pica. Madrid: Taurus Ediciones, 1961.
Con el viento solano. Barcelona: Editorial Planeta, 1956.
Cuaderno de godo. Madrid: Ediciones Arion, 1961.
Cuentos completos. Edited by Alicia Bleiberg. 2 vols. Madrid: Alianza, 1973.
El corazón y otros frutos amargos. Madrid: Ediciones Arion, 1959.
El fulgor y la sangre. Barcelona: Editorial Planeta, 1954.
El país vasco. Barcelona: Editorial Noguer, 1962.
Espera de tercera clase. Madrid: Ediciones Puerta del Sol, 1955.
Gran Sol. Barcelona: Editorial Noguer, 1957.
La tierra de nadie y otros relatos. Barcelona: Salvat Editores–Alianza Editorial, 1970.
Libro de las algas. Madrid: Talleres Gráficos CIES, 1949.
Los pájaros de Baden Baden. Madrid: Ediciones Cid, 1965.
Neutral Corner. Barcelona: Editorial Lumen, 1962.
Pájaros y espantapájaros. Madrid: Editorial Bullón, 1963.
Parte de una historia. Barcelona: Editorial Noguer, 1967.
Santa Olaja de acero y otras historias. Madrid: Alianza Editorial, 1968.
Todavía la vida. Madrid: Talleres Gráficos Argos, 1947.
Vísperas del silencio. Madrid: Taurus Ediciones, 1955.

2. Uncollected Articles, Notes, Reviews, and Stories

"A falta de 'filles' buenas son 'girls.' " *Guía,* March 1953, p. 7.
"Alava, provincia en cuarto menguante." *Clavileño* 4, no. 19 (January–February 1953), 66–69.
"Anécdota particular y nostálgica." *La Hora, número extraordianario,* 24 June 1950, p. 38.
"Bajo el 'Jolly Roger.' " *El Adelanto,* 22 February 1955, p. 6.
"Biografía de un mascarón de proa." *Revista de Pedagogía,* 9 July 1951, pp. 208–13.

"Carta de un estudiante a otro estudiante sobre materia postista." *El Español* 188 (1 June 1946), 3.

"Del surco al asfalto." *El Adelanto,* 14 April 1955, p. 6.

"Domador de incendios." *El Adelanto,* 30 November 1955, p. 6; also *El Diario Palentino,* 25 November 1955, p. 1.

"El ahogado." *Revista de Pedagogía,* nd.

"El arte de novelar." *Cuadernos Hispanoamericanos* 45 (September 1953), 401.

"El cuento en los Estados Unidos." Unpublished lecture notes.

"El Dostoiewsky de Castresana." *Cuadernos Hispanoamericanos* 54 (June 1954), 374–75.

"El herbolario y las golondrinas." *Juventud* 380 (22 February 1951), 6.

"El hombrecillo que nació para actor." *Juventud* 304 (8 September 1949), 3.

"El loro antillano." *La Hora* 54 (30 April 1950), 8.

"El mar de mi amigo Manuel Mampaso." *Guía,* December 1952, p. 18.

"El Palacio Real." *Reader's Digest* 29, no. 174 (May 1955).

"El teatro íntimo de doña Pom." *La Hora* 63 (1 October 1950).

"Función de aficionados." *La Hora* 68 (November 1950), 8.

"Gracia y teoría del EX-LIBRIS." *Trabajos y Días* 4, no. 11. (April–May 1949), 7.

"Hablando de *Escuadra hacia la muerte." Revista Española* 1 (May–June 1953), 119.

"Haciendo mutis." *El Diario Palentino,* 20 July 1955, p. 1.

"Haciendo tiempo." *Diario de Burgos,* 24 June, 1955; also *El Diario Palentino,* 25 June 1955, p. 1.

Interview with the director of the Student Theater Group at the University of Salamanca. *Cátedra,* no. 9 (March 1945), 14.

"La cerveza y la espada." *Guía,* February 1953, p. 18.

"La fantasma de Treviño." *La Hora* 59 (4 June 1950), 8.

"La farándula de la media legua." *La Hora* 8 (24 December 1948), 11.

"La 'Generación Beat.' " Unpublished lecture notes.

"La misma piedra." *Cuadernos Hispanoamericanos* 45 (September 1953), 398–401.

"La muerte de un curandero meteorólogo." *Correo Literario* 2, no. 19 (1 March 1951), 5.

"La sombra del marinero que estuvo en Singapur." *Bengala,* January–February 1951.

"Los novelistas jóvenes americanos." *Cuadernos Hispanoamericanos* 53 (May 1954), 235–36.

"Oscura noticia." *Guía,* August 1952.

"Panorama particular de la narrativa española de hoy." Unpublished lecture notes.

"Ponencia: universidad y gangsterismo." *Guía,* October 1952, p. 10.

"Por el mar de un piloto de altura." *Indice de Artes y Letras* 70–71

(January–February 1954), 28.

"¿Por qué gritan los mayores? Vago recuerdo del S.E.U. en el Instituto."
    La Hora 71 (26 November 1950), 9.

Prologue to *Escuela de Robinsones* by Jules Verne. Translated by Luis
    Alba de la Cuesta. Barcelona: Salvat, 1969. Pp. 9–13.

"Rapto de rey, consecuencia septiembre." *Guía,* July 1952, p. 13.

"Retrato de un mal estudiante de doce años." *Guía,* September 1952,
    p. 15.

Review of *El hombre es triste* by Marcelo Arroita Jáuregui. *Clavileño* 3,
    no. 15 (May–June 1952), 68.

Review of *Memorias íntimas de Aviraneta* by José Luis Castillo Puche.
    Cuadernos Hispanoamericanos 37 (January 1953), 98–100.

Review of *Requiem para una monja* by William Faulkner. *Cuadernos
    Hispanoamericanos* 47 (November 1953), 237–38.

Reviews of *El arpa de hierba* by Truman Capote and *Rápido tránsito* by
    José Coronel Urtecho. *Cuadernos Hispanoamericanos* 45 (September
    1953), 374–76.

"San Nicolás no sabe español." *Guía,* January 1953, p. 12.

"Sfax (tunicia) = Siesta (independencia)." *Guía,* June 1952.

"Trilogía: Hoffman, Núñez de Arce, Poe." *Cátedra,* no. 5 (January
    1944), 4.

"Un mar de historias." *Oficema* (Revista de Información de la Oficina
    Central Marítima), 7, no. 77 (December 1961), literary supplement.

"Urgente viaje de retorno." In *Alta Extremadura Libro de viaje.* Madrid:
    Departamento de Cultura, Delegación Nacional de Educación, 1956.
    Pp. 33–37.

"Viaje a Filabres." *Clavileño* 5, no. 27 (May–June 1954), 63–68.

"Walter Mitty y nosotros." *El Diario Palentino,* 27 October 1955, p. 1.

"Yo escribo de lo que tengo cerca, que es más bien triste." *La Estafeta
    Literaria* 42 (1956), 8.

SECONDARY SOURCES

1. Books

BORAU, PABLO. *El existencialismo en la novela de Ignacio Aldecoa.* Zara-
    goaz: Talleres Gráficos "La Editorial", 1974. In trying to force Alde-
    coa into the category of "existential realism" Borau does the author a
    disservice, but his interpretation of *With the East Wind* in particular
    is subtle and suggestive.

CARLISLE, CHARLES R. *Ecos del viento, silencios del mar: La novelística
    de Ignacio Aldecoa.* Madrid: Playor, 1976. Focusses on themes of
    loneliness and alienation in Aldecoa's novels, and studies the develop-
    ment to maturity of the author's lyrical prose style.

GARCÍA VIÑÓ, MANUEL. *Ignacio Aldecoa.* Madrid: Epesa, 1972. Collates important biographical and documentary information, imparts firm value judgments, but offers little in the way of interpretation of specific works.

LANDEIRA, RICARDO, and MELLIZO, CARLOS, eds. *Ignacio Aldecoa — A Collection of Critical Essays.* Laramie: University of Wyoming Press, Department of Modern and Classical Languages. 1977. Brings together some scholarly accounts of general and particular aspects of Aldecoa's work.

2. Articles and Essays

ABBOTT, JAMES H. "Ignacio Aldecoa and the Journey to Paradise (The Short Stories)." In *Ignacio Aldecoa — A Collection of Critical Essays,* pp. 59–68. Identifies a typological feature common to many of Aldecoa's stories.

ALBORG, JUAN LUIS. "Ignacio Aldecoa." In *Hora actual de la novela española.* Madrid: Taurus, 1958. Pp. 275–95. Sound appreciation of composition, characterization, and expressive resources in Aldecoa's first three novels and two volumes of stories.

ANON. "Ignacio Aldecoa: programa para largo." *Destino* 956 (3 December 1955), 37. In this, his first major interview with the national press, Aldecoa answers questions about his life and career as a writer, and defines his literary principles and aspirations.

ANON. "La técnica, la imagen, la palabra." *Griffith* 3 (December 1965), 4–10. Aldecoa and two other writers discuss the relation between literature and the cinema, in an interview which elicits some of his most profound remarks on the place of written and visual culture in Spanish society.

ANON. "Preguntas a Ignacio Aldecoa." *Indice de Artes y Letras* 132 (December 1959), 4. Aldecoa replies curtly to half a dozen questions about his place in Spanish fiction, the nature of his world view, and the extent of a writer's historical commitment.

ARROJO, FERNANDO. "Exactitud, economía y expresividad en la narrativa de Ignacio Aldecoa." *Explicación de textos literarios* 5, no. 1 (1976), 3–11. Documents Aldecoa's views on style, and suggests a literary pedigree extending from Cervantes and Quevedo to Henry James, Maupassant, and Camilo José Cela.

———. "El papel del mar en *Gran Sol:* Realidad y símbolo." In *Ignacio Aldecoa — A Collection of Critical Essays,* pp. 29–40. A reading of *Great Sole* alternately inspired and critical, the major value of which resides in Arrojo's ambition to establish a poetics of fiction for Aldecoa's work.

BRANDENBERGER, ERNA. *Estudios sobre el cuento español actual.* Madrid: Editora Nacional, 1973. Sets out to devise a methodology for evaluating the particularity of the short story in post–Civil War Spain. Confesses a debt to Aldecoa, often illustrating claims and conclusions with reference to his stories. Commentaries of "Ballad of the Manzanares" and "On the Fringe" deserve particular attention.

CARLISLE, CHARLES R. "Amos and Haggai: Sources of Thematic Motif and Stylistic Form in Ignacio Aldecoa's *Con el viento solano.*" *Bulletin of the Rocky Mountain Modern Language Association* 26 (Fall 1972), 83–88. An historically important article, being the first extended study in English of any single novel by Aldecoa. Examines biblical motifs and symbolic meaning in *With the East Wind,* but misconstrues Aldecoa's intentions from a standpoint of Christian doctrine.

CANO, JOSÉ LUIS. "Sigue el auge del cuento. Ignacio Aldecoa *Caballo de pica.* Francisco García Pavón *Cuentos republicanos.*" *Insula* 176–77 (July–August 1961), 12–13. Sensitive interpretation of the eleven stories in *The Picador's Mount,* based on the central image of the bullring.

DÍAZ, JANET WINECOFF. "The Novels of Ignacio Aldecoa." *Romance Notes* 11, no. 3 (1969), 475–82. An early introduction in English to the man and his work, setting both correctly in a historical and literary context.

———. "Amadís Existentialized: A Posthumous Tale by Ignacio Aldecoa." In *Ignacio Aldecoa: A Collection of Critical Essays,* pp. 103–13. A discriminating investigation of literary sources, and an examination of the author's critical intentions and strategy in this mature story.

DOMINGO, JOSÉ. "Ignacio Aldecoa *Santa Olaja de acero y otras historias.*" *Insula* 267 (February 1969), 5. Enthusiastic and perceptive review of this collection of stories.

ESPADAS, ELIZABETH. "Técnica literaria y fondo social del cuento 'A ti no te enterramos' de Ignacio Aldecoa." *Papeles de Son Armadans* 245–46 (August–September 1976), 163–73. An accurate appreciation of technique and rhetoric in this story.

FERNÁNDEZ ALMAGRO, MELCHOR. *"El fulgor y la sangre." ABC,* 3 April 1955, p. 51. An admirably objective assessment of Aldecoa's first novel.

FERNÁNDEZ BRASO, MIGUEL. "Ignacio Aldecoa levanta acta de los *Años de crisálida.*" *Indice de Artes y Letras* 236 (October 1968), 41–43. A further inquiry into the general foundations of Aldecoa's work, alluding to social implications, the influence of the cinema, and the state of the novel in Spain.

FIDDIAN, ROBIN. "Urban Man and the Pastoral Illusion in Ignacio Aldecoa's *Parte de una historia.*" *Revista de Estudios Hispánicos* 9 (October 1975), 371–89. Interprets *Parts of a Story* as an expression of the contemporary topos of the pastoral illusion.

———. "Interior Reduplication, Narrative Technique, and the Figure in the Carpet in Ignacio Aldecoa's *Parte de una historia.*" In *Ignacio Aldecoa: A Collection of Critical Essays,* pp. 49–57. Locates the literary specificity of *Part of a Story* in its symbolism and self-referentiality.

GARCÍA, IGNACIO. "Notas sobre una posible generación." *La Hora* 2 (12 November 1948), 24. Establishes criteria for membership of an emergent generation of writers in post–Civil War Spain.

GARCÍA PAVÓN, FRANCISCO. "Ignacio Aldecoa, novelista, cuentista." *Indice de Artes y Letras* 146 (February 1961), 4. Provides insights into Aldecoa's character, and distinguishes him from other writers of his generation by virtue of his sensibility and style.

GARCIASOL, RAMÓN DE. "*Vísperas del silencio.*" *Insula* 115 (July 1955), 6–7. Among the first of his commentators to regard Aldecoa as one who articulates a collective social concern for the humble and underprivileged.

GÓMEZ DE LA SERNA, GASPAR. "Un estudio sobre la literatura social de Ignacio Aldecoa." In *Ensayos sobre literatura social.* Madrid: Guadarrama, 1971. Pp. 67–210. Though moralistic in tone, the estimation offered of the spirit of Aldecoa's social commitment is fundamental to an understanding of the author's work. The study of the travel literature has yet to be superseded in quality and depth.

GRUPP, WILLIAM J. "Two Representatives of the Rising Young Generation of Spanish Novelists: José Luis Castillo Puche and Ignacio Aldecoa." *Kentucky Foreign Language Quarterly* 7, no. 2 (1960), 80–86. The author of this, the first survey in English of Aldecoa's novels and stories, accurately infers some general conclusions about their thematic and technical foundations.

JELINSKI, JACK B. "Ignacio Aldecoa: A Forgotten Master: A Critical Reexamination of *Gran Sol.*" In *Ignacio Aldecoa: A Collection of Critical Essays,* pp. 41–47. A keen examination of *Great Sole* both as artifact and expression of the author's personal world view, in which the themes of fate and fortune are justly highlighted.

LUIS, LEOPOLDO DE. A review of *Todavía la vida. Insula* 3, no. 30 (15 June 1948), iv. A perceptive response to Aldecoa's first volume of poetry.

MARRA LÓPEZ, JOSÉ RAMÓN. "*El corazón y otros frutos amargos,*" *Insula* 156 (November 1959), 6. A well-balanced appraisal of Aldecoa's achievements in *The Heart and Other Bitter Fruits.*

MARTÍN GAITE, CARMEN. "Apuntes urgentes para la biografía de un joven novelista. Un aviso: ha muerto Ignacio Aldecoa." *La Estafeta Literaria* 433 (1 December 1969), 4–7. An intimate account of Aldecoa's student years at Salamanca.

PÉREZ FIRMAT, GUSTAVO. "The Structure of *El fulgor y la sangre.*" *Hispanic Review* 45, no. 1 (Winter 1977), 1–12. In this penetrating analysis of *Blood and Lightning,* Pérez Firmat comments on the mechanisms of irony and suspense, and in a concluding aside suggests a typological reading of the women's situation as a reenactment of scenes from Greek tragedy.

PÉREZ MINIK, DOMINGO. "Conversación con Ignacio Aldecoa." In *Entrada y salida de viajeros*. Santa Cruz de Tenerife: Ediciones Nuestro Arte, 1969. Pp. 86–96. Limiting his attention to the second and fourth novels, Pérez Minik identifies the modernity of Aldecoa's conception of human existence and its particularity in a European context.

PERLADO, JOSÉ JULIO. "Ignacio Aldecoa escribe *Parte de una historia.*" *El Alcázar*, 3 May 1967, p. 21. Further coverage of the author's views on style, literary topics, and the distinctiveness of the short story. This interview records some unique declarations by Aldecoa about his intentions in *Part of a Story*.

PORCEL PUJOL, BALTASAR. "Una novela del mar." *Papeles de Son Armadans* 9, no. 26 (May 1958), 235–36. The author of this review of *Great Sole* comes close to perceiving the relation between Simón Orozco and Macario Martín.

RIDRUEJO, DIONISIO. "Presencia de Ignacio Aldecoa." *Destino* 35, no. 184 (14 April 1973), 41. In a review of Alicia Bleiberg's edition of the *Complete Stories*, Ridruejo remembers Aldecoa's personality, political attitudes, and literary qualities.

ROBERTS, GEMMA. "La decisión." In *Temas existenciales en la novela española de la postguerra*. Madrid: Gredos, 1973. Pp. 99–128. This closely argued, well-documented attempt to relate *With the East Wind* to the ideology of existentialism runs the risk of inflexibility but deserves close attention.

RODRÍGUEZ DE ALDECOA, JOSEFINA, ed. *Ignacio Aldecoa: Cuentos*. Madrid: Cátedra, 1977. Pp. 11–53. Aldecoa's widow gives an intimate, informative account of the background and inspiration of his work, and makes available an indispensable collection of theoretical declarations by and about Aldecoa.

SANTIAGO, MIGUEL DE. "Ignacio Aldecoa: una historia partida. Entrevista con Josefina Rodríguez." *La Estafeta Literaria* 578 (15 December 1975), 7–9. A revealing interview which touches on Aldecoa's life in the 1950s, his desire to revise topics in literature, his projected novel *Chrysalis Years*, and his attraction to dangerous and tragic themes.

SASTRE, ALFONSO. "Poco más que anécdotas 'culturales' alrededor de quince años (1950–1965)." *Triunfo, número extraordinario* 507 (17 June 1972), 81–85. A shrewd analysis of the political implications of literary activity in Spain in the 1950s.

SASTRE, LUIS DE. "La vuelta de Ignacio Aldecoa." *La Estafeta Literaria* 169 (15 May 1959), 23–24. Interviewing Aldecoa on his return from the United States, this reporter evinces succinct expressions of opinion about many issues, including the social usefulness of literature, the place of truth and authenticity in Aldecoa's literary credo, the nature of his "promoción," and his writing habits. Aldecoa also gives a retrospective summary of the essential features of his first three novels.

SENABRE, RICARDO. "La obra narrativa de Ignacio Aldecoa." *Papeles de Son Armadans* 15, no. 166 (1970), 5–24. Although he underestimates the complexity of Aldecoa's novelistic technique, Senabre has a sure appreciation of spirit and style in the stories.

————. "La técnica de la obertura narrativa en Ignacio Aldecoa." In *Ignacio Aldecoa: A Collection of Critical Essays,* pp. 95–101. A profitable commentary on the introduction to "Young Sánchez," emphasizing Aldecoa's mastery of significant detail and his overall technical skill.

SOBEJANO, GONZALO. *Novela española de nuestro tiempo.* Madrid: Editorial Prensa Española, 1970. Pp. 296–305. Sobejano recognizes the complex interrelation of social, existential, and mythic themes in, particularly, *With the East Wind* and *Great Sole.* His analyses of *Blood and Lightning* and *Part of a Story* are superficial in comparison.

————. "Sobre el arte descriptivo de Ignacio Aldecoa: *Con el viento solano.*" In *Ignacio Aldecoa: A Collection of Critical Essays,* pp. 17–27. An evaluation of the expressive effect of patterns of imagery and allusion in the second novel.

TRENAS, JULIO. "Así trabaja Ignacio Aldecoa." *Pueblo,* 5 October 1957, p. 11. Information about Aldecoa's early publications in the Spanish press, his attitude to poetry, plus some revealing comments about *Great Sole.*

3. Dissertations

FISCHER, OTTO. *La tragedia humilde en la narrativa de Ignacio Aldecoa.* Ph.D. dissertation, University of Miami, 1971. Sensitive discussion of the principal themes of loneliness, hardship, fate, and misfortune, that concludes with the affirmation of qualities of heroism and tragedy in Aldecoa's representation of man. Devotes valuable attention to Aldecoa's most neglected work, *Neutral Corner.*

LASAGABÁSTER MADINABEITIA, JESÚS M.ª *La novela de Ignacio Aldecoa De la mímesis al símbolo.* Madrid: Sociedad General Española de Librería, 1978. Examines the process of signification in Aldecoa's novels by distinguishing their mimetic, poetic, and symbolic functions.

Index

Agustí, Ignacio, 36

Alberti, Rafael, 43, 148

Aldecoa, Ignacio (1925–1969), and *postismo,* 18-19, 146; and the cinema, 29-30; and the Spanish Civil War, 13, 14-15, 16; collaboration in *Revista española,* 24; education, 13-15, 16-18; political attitude, 28-29; religious views, 14, 59; travel, 23, 25-26, 28

WORKS-MISCELLANEOUS:

Neutral Corner, 28, 37, 110, 140-43

"Sea of Tales, A" ("Un mar de historias"), 28, 42, 65, 83

"Short Story in the United States, The" ("El cuento en los Estados Unidos"), 39-40

WORKS-NOVELS:

Blood and Lightning (El fulgor y la sangre), 15, 21, 26, 37, 44-53, 55, 63-64, 65, 71, 109, 127, 156

Great Sole (Gran Sol), 21, 22, 26, 38, 64, 65-77, 83, 90, 92, 109, 156, 157

Part of a Story (Parte de una historia), 22, 27, 37, 78-90, 98, 120, 137, 149, 157

With the East Wind (Con el viento solano), 21, 26, 28, 30, 54-64, 88, 95, 111, 157

WORKS-POETRY:

Book of the Algae (Libro de las algas), 19, 148-54

"Footprints" ("Huellas"), 152-54

"Portraits" ("Retratos"), 151-52

Still Life Goes on (Todavía la vida), 19, 144-48

"Verses on the Joys of Wine" ("Versos de vino alegre"), 147

WORKS-STORIES:

"Aldecoa Has a Laugh" ("Aldecoa se burla"), 14, 125

"Amadís", 134-35

"Apprentice Conductor, The" ("El aprendiz de cobrador"), 94-95, 107

Archaeology (Arqueología), 26, 124-26, 135, 155

"Artist Called Pheasant, An" ("Un artista llamado Faisán"), 122-23

"Assassin, The" ("El asesino"), 124

"Assaults in Lime Village, The" ("Los atentados del barrio de la Cal"), 95

"At the 400 Kilometer Mark" ("En el kilómetro 400"), 109-10

"Ballad of the River Manzanares" ("Balada del Manzanares"), 116-17, 119

"Benito the Libelist" ("El libelista Benito"), 124-25, 126

"Between the Sky and the Sea" ("Entre el cielo y el mar"), 109

"Beyond the End of the Line" ("Tras de la última parada"), 111-12

"Biography of a Figurehead" ("Biografía de un mascarón de proa"), 91-92, 132, 149

"Bird of Paradise" ("Ave del paraíso"), 27, 42, 130-32, 156

Birds and Scarecrows (Pájaros y espantapájaros), 22, 26, 120-24, 135, 155

"Birds and Scarecrows, 123-24, 126

Birds of Baden Baden, The (Los pájaros de Baden Baden), 26, 127-34

"Birds of Baden Baden, The", 132-34

"Burning Sword, The" ("La espada encendida"), 116, 119

"Bus at 7:40, The" ("El autobús de las 7:40"), 105-106

176